D0113558

SERMONS ALIVE!

52
SHORT DRAMATIC
SKETCHES FOR
SUNDAY
WORSHIP

PAUL NEALE LESSARD

MERIWETHER PUBLISHING LTD.
Colorado Springs, Colorado

Meriwether Publishing Ltd., Publisher
Box 7710
Colorado Springs, CO 80933

Editor: Rhonda Wray
Typesetting: Sharon E. Garlock
Cover design: Tom Myers

© Copyright MCMXCIII Meriwether Publishing Ltd.
Printed in the United States of America
First Edition

All rights reserved. No part of this publication, except where specifically noted, may be reproduced, stored in a retrieval system, or transmitted, in any form or by any means, electronic, mechanical, photocopying, recording, or otherwise, without permission of the publishers. Permission to reproduce copies and perform any of the drama sketches included in this text is granted to amateur groups with the purchase of this book. Copies of these sketches and performance rights are for the purchaser and the purchasing organization only. These rights are not transferable to any other group or third party. These drama sketches may be produced by amateur groups without payment of a royalty fee. Permission for non-amateur presentation (professional stage, radio or television performances) must be obtained in writing from the publisher.

Scripture taken from the HOLY BIBLE, NEW INTERNATIONAL VERSION®. Copyright © 1973, 1978, 1984 by International Bible Society. Used by permission of Zondervan Publishing House. All rights reserved.

The "NIV" and "New International Version" trademarks are registered in the United States Patent and Trademark Office by International Bible Society. Use of either trademark requires the permission of International Bible Society.

Library of Congress Cataloging-in-Publication Data

Lessard, Paul Neale, 1960-
    Sermons alive! : 52 short dramatic sketches for Sunday worship / by Paul Neale Lessard.
       p.   cm.
    Includes indexes.
    ISBN 0-916260-95-X : $14.95
    1. Christian drama, American. 2. Drama in public worship.
I. Title.
PS3562.E8357S47   1993
812'.54--dc20   92-44911
                                                    CIP

Dedicated to
Tom Glossi, Jules Glanzer
and the
Fort Collins
Evangelical Covenant Church

FOREWORD

As producer for the music, comedy and drama group Jeremiah People, I'm really excited about what's been happening lately. Now don't tell anyone but they're starting to use the "D" word in churches now-a-days. DRAMA.

Yes, that's right, the idea of drama is finally coming into its own with verve and style. The phenomenal growth of churches like Willow Creek Community Church in suburban Chicago, Chapel Hill Harvester Church in Atlanta, and an increasing number of others that feature drama on a regular basis demonstrate its popularity. A short, well-acted sketch grabs the attention of a congregation and focuses it for the sermon that follows.

Whether your drama ministry is well established or fledgling, *Sermons Alive!* is a great resource for enhancing worship. There are 52 sketches included — one for every Sunday of the year. They are easy to do, they require no special lighting techniques or elaborate costumes, and they needn't be performed on a stage — the front of your sanctuary will work just fine.

Scripture and topical indexes are included so you can find an appropriate sketch to fit a particular sermon or worship service. *Sermons Alive!* zeroes in on themes that affect the church. You'll find scripts on giving ("Let's Make a Tithe Deal"), eternal life ("Forever Life Insurance"), commitment ("Christianity Lite"), peer pressure ("Raising a Dad"), faith ("Sewing 101"), and many other appropriate topics.

I hope you will use Paul Lessard's collection of witty, relevant sketches to move beyond the mindset that drama is just for Christmas, Easter, or other special occasions. Our goal with the Jeremiah People and Custer & Hoose is to express Christian truths in an enjoyable, approachable format. May you, too, utilize these sketches and realize that the "D" word is an effective vehicle for reminding your congregation of Christian truths, as taken from the pages of the Bible and applied to real life situations.

> — Bob Hoose
> Playwright
> Custer & Hoose Drama Duo
> Producer, Jeremiah People

TABLE OF CONTENTS

(All sketches are arranged in alphabetical order for easy reference.)

NOTE: The numerals running vertically down the left margin of each page of dialog are for the convenience of the director. With these he/she may easily direct attention to a specific passage.

INTRODUCTION

"You brood of vipers! Who warned you to flee from the coming wrath?" I sat transfixed as John the Baptist paced angrily back and forth across the front of the church, accusing me with his eyes. "Produce fruit in keeping with repentance." Those words of Luke's that seemed so distant and *safe* on the page were now seared across my mind. I could not avoid them. When the pastor returned to the podium to preach on the text that had just been so vividly communicated, I literally sat on the edge of my seat, waiting to hear what application he would make or what words of grace he might offer.

That was my first introduction to the use of drama in worship. I left church with the message of the morning ringing in my ears and the desire to play my part through drama burning in my heart. Since that time, I have had the chance to write, direct and perform sketches in worship practically every Sunday in the churches I have served in Texas and Colorado. I have been able to facilitate the use of drama in a wide variety of churches ranging from liturgical to charismatic, from traditional to contemporary. My experience has only reinforced in my mind how powerful drama can be in the context of our worship. A pulpit drama or a sketch in the service is a legitimate art form to enhance our understanding and appreciation of the great truths of our faith. If a picture is indeed worth a thousand words, then a picture that moves and talks and even on occasion interacts with us must be worth at least a million. How much more effective then to see that moving picture and not be bored or overwhelmed by the million words.

If the relaying of God's Word is important to us, then we would do well to use any means possible to communicate it. Drama is one of those means.

All of the sketches contained in this book were written for and used in worship. They were also written with the unchurched, the non-believer, and biblically illiterate in mind. These are the same people that the church was attempting to reach when it first introduced drama to worship in the late 10th Century. As I continue to use drama in worship, I am often reminded that few of the elements of our worship services can be understood by both children and adults, teens and unchurched friends, new and mature believers. Not everything should relate to the lowest common denominator, but some elements in our worship should be easily understood by most of those attending, or we are guilty of catering to an elite few who speak a very special language. Drama can span the many differences found among

1

the people of our worshiping communities. A well-written drama, based on the Scripture or teaching theme for the morning, can pull a service together. It can set up the question that the pastor intends to answer and it can bring focus to the theme of the sermon. It can serve as a mnemonic device, a way of remembering what was said and done in worship. You will find that drama is something that entire families can understand. They will discuss the morning's sketch in the car on the way home. In short, it is a powerful communication tool that is available at little cost, and is relatively easy to put together.

Most churches will find it easier to gather a group of actors than to form a choir. Many people who have a hard time speaking in public find it quite another matter to "play" someone else. Some of my strongest actors over the years have been classic introverts who came alive on stage when given the chance to portray a character. Drama then becomes a two-fold ministry: it enhances the quality of your worship service as well as providing an area of service for the actors themselves. In one of the churches I served, we had over 60 different people involved in our worship in one year through acting in the dramas — and that didn't count the Christmas and Easter productions. Many people have the ability and the desire to serve if given the opportunity. To start using drama in worship is to provide yet another area of meaningful service in your church.

GETTING IT ALL TOGETHER

The following helps for producing a drama in worship are written as if you are directing. You may be acting as well, but unless someone assumes the role of director, your sketches run the risk of looking amateurish and unfocused.

Rehearsal

The majority of the sketches in this book (help outlaw the use of the word "skits" for sketches in worship) can be memorized and rehearsed in about two hours' time. A typical schedule of preparation should look like this:

1. Decide on the sketch to be used.
2. Line up your actors at least five days in advance of the worship service you are preparing for (don't line them up too far in advance as they won't memorize until the night before the rehearsal anyway).
3. As you line up your actors, set a one-hour rehearsal time with them immediately. (Have your rehearsal a day or two before the worship service.)

4. Meet early enough before the service to run through the sketch a couple of times.

A one-hour rehearsal will allow you to work on memorization and blocking as a group. If your actors have given some time to memorizing the sketch beforehand, you will find that an hour is plenty. Many ongoing pulpit drama ministries actually do not rehearse until the Sunday morning prior to the worship service. However, it is best to have a strong ministry in place with reliable people of proven ability before rehearsing that close to the actual performance. When you present a drama to your congregation for the first time, make sure you have rehearsed and rehearsed and rehearsed. Don't leave anything to chance.

Tweaking

Many sketches written for worship may need to be "tweaked" or modified somewhat to fit your theme or topic better. Some of the sketches in this book will allow you to insert the name of your pastor, local stores, and local geographical features, such as rivers, lakes or highways. This helps to make the sketches more personal and relevant. Often the same sketch can fit a number of different themes or Scriptures, and simply by changing a Scripture reference or the narration, the sketch can serve to support the topic even better. Make sure you understand the sketch, its humor and how it builds before you change too much, but tweak as needed to fit your situation.

Many of the sketches in this book are not gender specific and the roles are interchangeable. In other words, if you have two men and the sketch was written for two women, it may not be critical to the story that the characters be female. However, if you do change the gender of a character, be sure to change the name and any relevant costuming.

Terminology

Some of the words contained in the directions for these sketches may be new to you. Here is a simple guide:

Freeze — At the end of the sketch, after the last line is said, the actors freeze or become motionless for about five seconds. This is like the period at the end of the sentence. It says that the drama is over. The Freeze is a convention that has grown out of doing theatre in places that do not have a curtain.

Blocking, Block — When you figure out where everyone will be located on the platform and how they will move during the sketch, you are blocking. Do not leave anything to chance. Know where everyone will enter and exit. Know where the actors will stand and sit. Know when they will pick up the phone or pound their fist on the table. Everything must be decided before or during the rehearsal.

Narrator — The Narrator reads a clarifying or introductory statement but is not one of the actors in the sketch. The Narrator may be off to one side or sitting in the front pew, but should stand and address the congregation when reading the part. If the narration is at the end of the sketch, the Narrator must be prepared to do his/her part just as soon as the actors freeze.

Directing

The director's job is to oversee all the different aspects in putting a sketch together. You find out the theme from the pastor, determine how much time you have to fill, find the script, line up the actors, set the rehearsal times and try to both encourage your actors as well as give them helpful feedback. One of your main tasks is to attempt to view the sketch as the congregation would. This is true in a physical sense (Can I see the actor's face?) and also in a conceptual sense (Do I understand what is happening or being said here?).

Obviously there are many excellent books written on directing. The more directing experience you have, the better your dramas will communicate. However, if you are aware of the following three basic areas, you shouldn't have any trouble blocking and performing your first sketch. I call these the three Vs — Voice, Visibility and Veracity.

Voice — Is the voice loud enough? Can you hear all that is being said? Are your actors doing strange things with their voices? Are they using an affected accent? Are they shouting? Are they swallowing their words? Are their voices higher than normal, squeaky, indistinct, muffled, lifeless or trembling? Words are very important to drama, but especially so in the church where we really care about what is being said. Make sure that every word is clear, distinct and full of life.

Visibility — Can you see the actors' faces? Are they showing their backs too much? When they sit down, do they disappear from sight? Is there any furniture in the way? Are any of the actors blocking the view of the rest of the actors? Can you see all the things they are supposed to be doing? Can you see more than just their heads? When two actors speak to each other, they needn't face one another. They can "cheat out." This is accomplished by their bodies being turned out to the congregation, but their faces turned toward each other. When we can see the front of the body, we read more body language.

Veracity (truthfulness) — Are the actors believable? Are they acting well enough that you suspend disbelief and allow yourself to get caught up in the story? Trust your gut reactions here. Be wary of doing serious drama with people who do not have the emotional depth to carry it off. If a character in a sketch needs to cry, make sure it is believable, or it becomes a parody of real emotion. If a character needs to be angry, make sure he comes across as genuinely angry. Your actors must commit to the part. They must play the character without reservation. If the actors hold back, they will never completely draw the congregation into the story. During the rehearsal process, you, as director, must give this feedback so that they know how they are being perceived. Encourage your actors as to how to make their characters more believable.

Staging

In pulpit dramas, minimal staging is best. In fact, it is preferred. Most of the time all you will need is a stool, maybe a little table, or an exercise bike, maybe a sewing machine, and the occasional hat or jacket. A cup and saucer can be mimed, as can a water hose. In general, have only those props or set pieces that are absolutely necessary to the sketch. If the props and set pieces are well chosen, they also become symbols for whatever point the sketch is making. A simple setup like a telephone sitting on top of a stool creates expectation and speaks to the greater meaning of the sketch. If you become too complicated with your set, prop and costume choices, you run the risk of detracting from and even over-shadowing the message of your material. Do not let your props or set pieces become a distraction in worship. Full set pieces, lights and Elizabethan costuming may not only damage the focus of your worship, but it can be rather pretentious for a three-minute sketch.

Stage in such a way that you do not compete with the worship space but rather compliment and enhance what is there. Strive for a clean look that creates an image that you will color in with your sketch. Make sure, however, that you have the props that are necessary for a good understanding of the sketch. Not everything can be mimed to equal effect.

Memorizing

First-time actors can be quite worried about memorization. The first principle of memorization is to be familiar with the entire sketch. If your actors know what the story is about, then the lines make more sense. It is generally easier to memorize when someone prompts a line by reading it and then you respond with your line. Some of my actors record the sketch on cassette tape, leaving space for their responses. Usually in the process of working the sketch a few lines at a time during the rehearsal, the actors will memorize their lines with little effort. If they consistently stumble on the same line, back up and work through the section repeatedly. Any lines that are consistently dropped (forgotten), turned around or mispronounced during rehearsal will happen the same way during performance unless you take steps to correct it.

As with most new endeavors, the best way to learn how to do something is often to just do it. Your directing ability and skill as an actor will improve with time if you are willing to reflect on your performances, critique yourself and your actors, and take constructive criticism. If your goal is to communicate the truths of God, then you will want your dramatic skills to be the best they can be. Others may have helpful ideas for you.

Most churches are very open to the idea of drama in worship. If those involved in the planning and implementation of the worship services feel they can trust you, they will welcome your participation in this way. You will have a "window of opportunity," and you must make the most of it. As mentioned above, rehearse, rehearse and rehearse again. Do not leave anything to chance. If your sketch goes well, with the material being appropriate and complementary to the service, the congregation will want more.

Where in Worship?

A sketch can be placed most anywhere in the order of worship. The drama can express those elements of worship that we seek to express with our music, readings, prayers and preaching. I have used dramas as calls to worship, to introduce the Scripture reading, to respond to the reading of Scripture, to prepare for the offering, as a preparation for confession, as a statement of responsibility, as an illustration prior to the preaching or homily, as an illustration in the middle of the sermon, as a response to the pastor's message, and finally as a benediction. Just as we would use special music or the choir most anywhere in our service depending on the song and theme, so I have used drama depending on its message and tone. Like responsive readings, spontaneous prayers, and music, drama can be another means of expression. Be creative. The better the drama fits in the context of the worship service, the more your congregation will see it as being a valuable part of its language of worship.

Doing drama in worship is just plain fun! It truly is one area of service that can recharge you as you give of your time and abilities. I wish you good luck as you begin or continue to use drama in your worship. I hope this book contributes to your enjoyment of your ministry as much as to its strength.

All I Want for Christmas

THEME: **Christmas** — What our world really needs for Christmas is not found in the catalogs.

SCRIPTURE: **Luke 2:14** — " 'Glory to God in the highest, and on earth peace to men on whom his favor rests.' "

SYNOPSIS: While making up her Christmas list, a woman realizes that what she really wants for Christmas can only be given by the Christ Child. As she tells us her story, we see three vignettes that explain how she came to her conclusion.

CHARACTERS: Lori — main character
Husband
Wife
Mugger
Victim — preferably male
Doctor

COSTUMES: Winter coat and gloves for Lori, stained white lab coat for the Doctor, suit jacket with interior breast pocket for the Victim, and possibly a black leather jacket for the Mugger.

PROPS: Sears Wishbook catalog, big box of diapers, a phone (could be mimed).

SETTING: Divide the stage into two playing areas. One side is Lori's home. On that side, place a stool or high table and set the Sears catalog on it. On top of the catalog, place the box of diapers. The other side of the stage is bare — it is used for the three vignettes.

1   *(Scene opens with LORI putting on a winter coat and a pair of*
2   *gloves. She is getting ready to head outside.)*
3 **LORI:** *(Humming as she puts on coat and gloves. Addresses*
4   *audience.)* **Do I look like I'm going out to do some Christmas**
5   **shopping? It's about time I gave some thought to that,**
6   **but I'm not buying presents tonight.** *(Picks up the box of*
7   *diapers.)* **Actually, I'm going to do some Christmas giving.**
8   **You're probably thinking that this is a pretty lousy**
9   **Christmas gift. Diapers are not very sentimental now,**
10   **are they?** *(Pause)*
11   **Do you remember how when you were young what**
12   **you** *gave* **for Christmas was sometimes tied to what you**
13   *wanted* **for Christmas? When I was eight, I wanted a set**
14   **of walkie-talkies so bad that I lay awake at night thinking**
15   **about how I could get a pair. Then, two weeks before**
16   **Christmas, my mom gave me money to buy a present for**
17   **my three-year-old sister. I knew exactly what to get her —**
18   **a pair of walkie-talkies.** *(Looks at the diapers.)* **Sometimes**
19   **what we give says a lot about what we want.** *(Sets diapers*
20   *down.)*
21   **About this time last year, after wrestling my kids to**
22   **bed, I finally sat down in my reading chair to make up**
23   **my Christmas list. In our family, we make a list of ten**
24   **things that we would like and then put the list on the**
25   **fridge. The kids had had their lists up since, oh, probably**
26   **the beginning of September, but on this night, just three**
27   **weeks before Christmas, I was finally putting my list**
28   **together.**
29   **I really hadn't given much thought to what I wanted,**
30   **so I got myself comfortable with a cup of tea, carols on**
31   **the radio and a fire in the fireplace. I had the Sears**
32   **Wishbook to browse through for ideas and I had a pad**
33   **of paper to write my list on. But when I opened the**
34   **Wishbook,** *(She opens catalog and flips through it as she talks)*
35   **I was amazed to see that my children had gone through**

1 the entire catalog page by page, circling and underlining
2 everything they wanted. They had each used a different
3 color so I wouldn't mistake who wanted which gift. The
4 Sears Wishbook was one big wish list for my family.
5 Initially I flipped through the catalog, amused at
6 the high hopes and great expectations shown by my kids,
7 and even my husband in a few cases, but after awhile I
8 began to feel uneasy. Of course they didn't expect to get
9 everything that they asked for, but they wanted so much, so
10 much. All the things that they were asking for were typical —
11 toys and games that most kids want, but I began to
12 understand the circled items as being symbolic in some way.
13 One of my kids circled a supermarket set. You've
14 probably seen it. It comes with a shopping cart and a
15 check-out stand complete with a shelf full of pretend
16 groceries. Seeing all that food triggered something in me
17 and suddenly I was overwhelmed with thoughts of all
18 the hunger in this world. *(Freeze as first vignette is played out.)*
19
20   VIGNETTE 1
21
22 **DOCTOR:** *(Enters with phone, paces as he talks. He is very tired*
23   *and quite exasperated.)* **What do you mean that's all you can**
24   **send? . . . What? What? I can't hear you . . . Of course we**
25   **need more! Yesterday alone we had four hundred thirty-**
26   **one die . . . What? Speak up! Half children, all Somalians**
27   **except for one crazy American who refused to eat more**
28   **than the refugees were getting . . . Yes,** *send more food . . .*
29   *(Sarcastic)* **Yeah, yeah . . . well, he probably has more food**
30   **in his garbage than we've got in the entire village . . . Yes,**
31   **yes . . . OK, OK, just tell them to please do what they can,**
32   **and hurry . . .** *(Freeze and then LORI's voice changes the focus*
33   *allowing the character to exit.)*
34
35 **LORI:** I turned the page and saw that one of my kids had

1 **underlined, circled and highlighted with big yellow stars**
2 **a video game called "Street Fighter."** *(Thoughtfully)* **The**
3 **picture showed three tough-looking guys chasing down**
4 **a fellow in a business suit** ... *(Freeze as second vignette is*
5 *played out.)*
6 **VIGNETTE 2**
7
8 *(VICTIM enters and walks across the stage. MUGGER starts*
9 *from the back of the sanctuary and runs up the aisle, coming up*
10 *behind the VICTIM. This should happen very quickly. The*
11 *MUGGER must be very intense and threatening in an*
12 *understated way. The VICTIM must look terrified.)*
13 **MUGGER:** *(Sticks his hand in VICTIM's back like he has a gun.*
14 *He frisks the VICTIM as he speaks.)* **OK, stand very still and**
15 **don't move. You'll be on your way in no time at all.**
16 *(VICTIM moves when the MUGGER finds the wallet in the breast*
17 *pocket of his jacket. Very intensely, clenched teeth and*
18 *tremendous hostility)* **I said don't move! What's the matter,**
19 **tired of living?** *(He gets the wallet.)* **OK, don't you move or**
20 **I'll be back** ... *(MUGGER backs away, watching the man and*
21 *then runs Off-stage. The man puts his hand to his face and*
22 *begins to sob silently and freezes. When LORI begins to speak*
23 *he exits quickly.)*
24
25 **LORI:** *(Pensive)* **I kept paging through the catalog, feeling**
26 **more and more troubled. In a strange sort of way, I was**
27 **beginning to get an idea of what I wanted for Christmas.**
28 **Then, at the very end of the Wishbook, I saw the last**
29 **circled present. My youngest wanted three dolls — a**
30 **family: a mommy, a daddy and a baby. All the dolls were**
31 **smiling — they looked so happy.**
32
33 **VIGNETTE 3**
34
35 **HUSBAND:** *(Angrily)* **You have no right to talk to me that way.**

10

1   **Do you hear? I make the rules around here.**
2   **WIFE:** *(Just as angry)* **You make the rules? You make the**
3   **rules? Then I guess you found something you can finally do.**
4   **HUSBAND:** *(Warningly)* **Don't start on that.**
5   **WIFE:** **Hey, if I didn't start things, nothing would ever get**
6   **done around here. If we waited for *you* to do anything,**
7   **we would starve to death!** *(She turns and begins to walk away.)*
8   **HUSBAND:** *(Right at the edge)* **Don't push me — don't push me!**
9   *(Takes a threatening step toward her and spins her around to*
10   *face him. Freeze. Exit when LORI begins to speak.)*
11
12   **LORI:** *(Softly)* **I closed the Wishbook** *(Closes catalog)* **and sat**
13   **in silence for a long time. It made my heart ache to think of**
14   **what I really wanted for Christmas. What I wanted could**
15   **not be found in a catalog or in a store. I needed a Wishbook**
16   **all right, but one filled with gifts of love, peace, and joy that**
17   **I could give away. So I made my list, and this is what I**
18   **wanted for Christmas last year: I wanted everyone to have**
19   **full stomachs. I wanted people to feel safe and not be abusive**
20   **to each other. I wanted husbands and wives, children and**
21   **parents to care for one another and have relationships built**
22   **on love and respect.**
23   **When I finished my list, it became clear to me that if**
24   **these were the things that I wanted for Christmas, then**
25   **maybe these were the same things I should give. Remember,**
26   **what we give can say a lot about what we want. So I decided**
27   **to give the gift that God gave us: the Christ Child. I thought**
28   **that if I gave of myself in some small way, that I might help**
29   **bring his peace and love and care into someone else's life —**
30   **the same peace, love and care that the Christ Child has given**
31   **me. So I've been helping this past year at a home for teenage**
32   **mothers.** *(Picks up diapers.)* **That's why I'm off with a box of**
33   **diapers.** *(Turns to leave.)* **Oh, if you're interested, my new**
34   **Christmas list is already up on the fridge. I'm asking for the**
35   **same things again this year. Merry Christmas!** *(Freeze)*

Back to Back With Benny

THEME: **Christian Lifestyle** — The words of Jesus present a picture of who we should be. They are the standard against which we measure ourselves.

SCRIPTURE: **Matthew 5-7** — The Sermon on the Mount.

SYNOPSIS: In a monolog, a Jewish woman tells us about her kids and how they measure their growth against their father. She then draws a parallel to our growth measured against the words of Jesus.

CHARACTERS: Martha — Mother of seven children. (Martha should be played with a touch of humor as she is somewhat self-pitying.)

COSTUMES: None necessary. Biblical robe optional.

PROPS: Sewing needle, pile of clothes, and a worn T-shirt.

SETTING: Biblical times. Sketch takes place in Martha's home. Set a chair Center Stage by the pile of clothes.

1   *(Scene opens with MARTHA sitting behind the stack of clothes*
2   *sewing intently.)*
3   **MARTHA:**   Oy vey... *(Big sigh)* **Washing and mending,**
4   **mending and washing, that's all I ever seem to do. You**
5   **give 'em clean clothes and they just get them dirty. Might**
6   **as well go naked, I say! Washing and mending. I**
7   **remember Benny saying to me, "Marry me, Martha, and**
8   **you'll see things you never knew existed!" Well, after**
9   **seven children, I can honestly say, "Benny, that's one**
10   **thing you were right about." Oy vey** ... *(Big sigh)*
11   **All these clothes with holes in them** ... **The kids**
12   **wear them out faster than I can mend them.** *(Holds up a*
13   *well-worn T-shirt.)* **I think all four boys wore this shirt.**
14   **First Matthew,** *(Not too fast so the audience gets the joke)* **and**
15   **then Mark, then Luke wore it for awhile, and now** *(Slight*
16   *pause)* **Francis wears it. The girls all wear hand-me-downs**
17   **too. I sew something for Mary, and before you know it,**
18   **Maria is wearing it, and finally Miriam. Oy vey** ... *(Big*
19   *sigh)* **Kids** ... **they grow so fast.**
20   **They all like to measure their height against their**
21   **father, Benny. He is the standard. Of course Benny really**
22   **doesn't have much height — he has more width than**
23   **anything. Oy vey** ... *(Big sigh)* **But they stand back to**
24   **back with Benny and then we mark their heights on the**
25   **door post. Mary is the tallest — she is almost three cubits.**
26   **They all look at their dad and say, "I could be that tall**
27   **some day." Except maybe Francis. I think he looks at**
28   **Benny and thinks, "someday I could be that wide." Well,**
29   **whatever. I sometimes think that if they didn't know how**
30   **tall they could be, they wouldn't worry about it; they**
31   **would be satisfied the way they are.** *(She picks up another*
32   *piece of clothing to mend.)* **Oy vey** ... *(Big sigh)*
33   **This is kind of like what's been happening around**
34   **here with this fella Jesus. He's been trying to show us a**
35   **new standard for living. He says the old ways of measuring**

whether or not one is a good person aren't enough anymore. Just when I thought I wasn't half bad, I find out I'm only half good. Oy vey . . . *(Big sigh)* Jesus says things like, "Happy are the pure in heart, for they will see God." [1] *(To herself)* I wonder, if my heart is only partly pure, will I only see a part of God? *(Shrugs her shoulders.)*

Hmmm . . . Jesus has been telling us to not resist an evil person and to love our enemies. He says, "Don't worry about treasure on earth — store it up in heaven." [2] I want to say to him, "Tell me the address for heaven and I'll take my treasure and store it there myself!" Oy vey . . . *(Big sigh)* No doubt about it, Jesus is setting a new standard. And, when I measure myself against his words, I get worried; I'm not very tall when I stand back to back with Jesus. *(Shakes her head.)* I don't know. Oy vey . . . *(Big sigh)* but I think that although Jesus' way is harder, it may be better. We'll see. *(Resumes mending and then holds up the shirt.)* There we go, good as secondhand. *(Freeze)*

[1] *Paraphrase of Matthew 5:8*
[2] *Paraphrase of Matthew 5:19, 20*

A Ball Game

THEME: **Learning** — God can make successes from our failures if we learn from our mistakes.

SCRIPTURE: **Romans 8:28** — "In all things God works for the good of those who love him . . ."

SYNOPSIS: Two boys learn that losing a ball game can actually make them better ball players. In the same way, God can bring success out of failure in the lives of Christians. This sketch applies to all ages but may be especially good for junior highers.

CHARACTERS: Tyler — A junior high aged baseball player
Kevin — Same as above
Narrator

COSTUMES: Baseball uniforms or athletic apparel.

PROPS: Two ball gloves and a baseball.

SETTING: Outside — a ball park.

"I can't believe we lost the game!"

1   NARRATOR: In the New Testament it says that, "In all things
2   God works for the good of those who love him, who have
3   been called according to his purpose." [1] If our lives are
4   committed to God, then he can bring positive results out
5   of the negative events life can throw our way. With God,
6   success *can* come out of failure. *(Enter TYLER and KEVIN*
7   *looking dejected, slamming their fists into their gloves, etc.)*
8   TYLER: I can't believe we lost the game!
9   KEVIN: Well, they did outplay us . . .
10   TYLER: Kevin, you mean they outplayed me! I played
11   terrible. We lost the game because of me.
12   KEVIN: Tyler, we all played bad tonight . . .
13   TYLER: Yeah, I guess so.
14   KEVIN: But you probably played the worst!
15   TYLER: Thanks a lot! I'll never make it as a ball player.
16   KEVIN: Do you know what you did wrong?
17   TYLER: I sure do! I've been going over all the errors in my
18   mind. I know what I'd do different if I had another
19   chance!
20   KEVIN: But you do have another chance.

1   TYLER: I do?

2   KEVIN: Sure, tomorrow night.

3   TYLER: But I want another chance at the game we lost

4   tonight!

5   KEVIN: Tyler, what's done is done, but tonight's game

6   doesn't have to be a total loss.

7   TYLER: What do you mean?

8   KEVIN: Well, if you know what you did wrong, then learn

9   from your mistakes and play a better game tomorrow

10   night.

11   TYLER: Give me a break — that sounds like something my

12   dad would say!

13   KEVIN: Remember when you learned to ride a bike?

14   TYLER: Yes, I was just a little kid.

15   KEVIN: Did you fall off?

16   TYLER: *(Sarcastically)* What do you think?

17   KEVIN: Well, when you got back up on your bike you knew

18   what *not* to do, right?

19   TYLER: Yeah.

20   KEVIN: So you learned from your mistakes. It's the same

21   with the ball game.

22   TYLER: I see what you're saying. We lost tonight, but

23   because of it, we could play better tomorrow

24   night . . . and win!

25   KEVIN: You got it! Losing's still a bummer, but when you

26   think about tomorrow's game, it doesn't seem like such

27   a big deal.

28   TYLER: It kind of makes you wish you'd made more mistakes,

29   doesn't it? *(KEVIN gives TYLER a "You've got to be kidding"*

30   *look and they both freeze.)*

31   NARRATOR: If we learn from our mistakes and failures, the

32   Lord can better use us for his purpose. Success can come

33   from failure.

34

35   *¹ Romans 8:28*

The Bible Study

THEME: **Encouragement** — We should be looking for more opportunities to encourage one another to good works and love.

SCRIPTURE: **Hebrews 10:24-25** — "Let us consider how we may spur one another on toward love and good deeds . . . let us encourage one another."

SYNOPSIS: Two couples who have been meeting regularly for a Bible study realize that they have not been encouraging each other to apply what they have been studying.

CHARACTERS: Sally
Jeff
Tom
Donna
Narrator

COSTUMES: Casual attire.

PROPS: Bible study books, Bibles.

SETTING: A small group Bible study. This sketch is in Readers Theatre format so it may be simply staged (as in four stools on a bare stage).

"Let's encourage each other to live our faith out."

1   **NARRATOR:**   This is the story
2   **of couples who meet**
3   **each week for small group and**
4   **they're faithful to keep**
5
6   **Each Wednesday for group time**
7   **but not quite as apt**
8   **to let the Lord show them**
9   **the course he has mapped.**
10
11   **But tonight may be different**
12   **for Sally's in doubt.**
13   **God's prodding her conscience —**
14   **she needs to speak out.**
15
16   **JEFF:**   Well, Tom, thanks a lot,
17   **the study was great.**
18   **Thanks for thinking things through**
19   **SALLY:**   *(With a laugh)* **And setting us straight.**
20   **DONNA:**   It's not just *his* doing . . .

1   TOM: *(Apologetically)* **I can't do it all.**

2   **I admit some of my thoughts . . .**

3   SALLY: **. . . came from Charles Swindoll?** *(They all laugh.)*

4   JEFF: **Well, even if the study**

5   **was prepared in great haste,**

6   **Tom always has jokes,**

7   **so it's never a waste.**

8   TOM: *(Earnestly)* **I believe if we read**

9   **just *one* word of the text,**

10   **God will honor our study**

11   **And lives will be blessed,**

12   DONNA: *(Sweetly)* **'cause we care enough**

13   **to spend time together,**

14   JEFF: **to think on his words,**

15   TOM: **and to pray with each other.**

16   SALLY: *(Reluctantly)* **Uh, I have to admit**

17   **I've been troubled of late,**

18   **though the fellowship's good**

19   **and the food's always great.**

20

21   **But shouldn't there be more**

22   **than just fun and games?**

23   **God wants us to grow**

24   **and not stay the same.**

25   ALL: *(Silence — they look over their books and stare at her.)*

26   JEFF: *(Nervous laugh)* **Hey, uh, Thomas, my friend,**

27   **did you happen to see**

28   **those brand new Ford vans**

29   **I sold to the city?**

30   TOM: **Why, yes, Jeff, I have!**

31   **And if you ask me**

32   **what a terrible waste**

33   **of taxpayers' money.**

34

35   **In fact . . .**

1	DONNA: Now hold on, you two!
2	Didn't you hear
3	what Sally was saying
4	'bout the time we spend here?
5	
6	She asked a hard question
7	and she just may be right.
8	Do we see our lives change
9	as we meet Wednesday nights?
10	TOM: *(Pontificates)* Well, now, change is something
11	that is so hard to gauge,
12	it's sanctification ...
13	JEFF: *(Trying to be helpful)* ... and spiritual age.
14	
15	Dear, you just can't take
16	Tom and Donna to task.
17	Your growth is *our* business —
18	it's not fair to ask
19	
20	that they be responsible
21	for what's troubling you.
22	SALLY: But, do we really care
23	what God wants us to do?
24	
25	I've been reading in Hebrews
26	which makes it quite clear
27	that our lives should be changing
28	from spending time here.
29	TOM: Now, where does it say
30	we're not doing enough?
31	We live under grace!
32	Don't make faith so tough.
33	DONNA: When it comes to our growth,
34	we've got the Big Three ...
35	SALLY: I know, *(Checks them off on her fingers)*

1	**Bible and prayer,**
2	**and decaf coffee.**
3	
4	**But what of encouragement?**
5	**DONNA:** *(Emphatic agreement)* **That we could use.**
6	**JEFF:** *(To SALLY, rather snide)* **Dear! What a nice dress,**
7	**TOM:** *(Patronizing)* **It's so slimming on you!**
8	**SALLY:** **No, you guys,**
9	**that's not what I mean.**
10	**Let me read you the Scripture**
11	**and see if you glean**
12	
13	**the same meaning as I**
14	**when I first read it through.**
15	**It's not easy to hear this —**
16	*(Looks imploringly at TOM and JEFF)* **and it's hard for me, too.**
17	
18	*(Pause. SALLY reads from a Bible.)*
19	
20	**"Encourage each other**
21	**to love and good deeds."** [1]
22	*(She looks up at her friends.)* **You see, we don't pray about**
23	**each other's needs.**
24	
25	**Let's encourage each other**
26	**to live our faith out —**
27	**to practice what's studied**
28	**is what it's about.**
29	
30	**To take what we're learning**
31	**and apply it to life.**
32	**That's where we need help —**
33	**JEFF:** *(Hastily jumps in)* **— let me explain my wife.**
34	
35	*[1] Paraphrase of Hebrews 10:24*

1   She's been reading in James
2   and it's caused her to dread.
3   It says, "Faith by itself,
4   without action, is dead." [2]
5 SALLY: Let's start to encourage
6   each other along.
7   Let's better our friendship —
8   Let's make it strong!
9 TOM: Well, it's just like you say —
10   the Scripture is clear,
11 DONNA: and it doesn't leave room
12   for complacency here.
13 TOM: I really don't know
14   if that's how I can be,
15   but God calls us to live
16   with integrity.
17 JEFF: To spur one another
18   to good works and love
19   means stronger commitment.
20 SALLY: ... with help from above.
21
22   This isn't just something
23   we do on our own.
24 DONNA: If we apply what we know
25   our faith will be shown.
26 TOM: Perhaps they *will* know
27   We're Christians by our love.
28 DONNA: *(Shaking her head ruefully)* Not through my bad coffee ...
29 ALL: *That* needs help from above!
30 NARRATOR: So, after the study, the four joined in prayer
31   and asked God to give them all hearts full of care.
32   To encourage each other to do more than talk,
33   but to live out their faith and put feet to their walk.
34
35 [2] *Paraphrase of James 2:17*

The Bonsai Tree

THEME: **Growth** — God shapes our lives to make us more like Jesus.

SCRIPTURE: **Isaiah 64:8** — "We are the clay, you are the potter; we are all the work of your hand."

SYNOPSIS: Two friends discover that pruning and shaping a bonsai tree is similar to how God prunes and shapes us. In both cases the "gardener" knows what he/she wants the "plant" to look like.

CHARACTERS: Ann
Sue
(Two friends)

COSTUMES: Casual "Saturday" clothes.

PROPS: Bonsai tree, spray bottle, and miscellaneous gardening tools for house plants.

SETTING: Sue's house.

"Well, it hurts to be pruned."

1   *(Scene opens with SUE intent upon pruning her bonsai tree. This*
2   *is done by pinching the ends of the branches. ANN enters.)*
3   ANN: Hi, Sue, am I too early to stop by for a cup of coffee?
4   SUE: Hi, Ann, not at all. I'm just about finished here.
5   ANN: That tree is sure pretty. How come it's so small?
6   SUE: It's because of the way it's pruned. You actually pinch
7   off the ends to shape it and make it look the way you want.
8   ANN: You know how you want that tree to look?
9   SUE: I sure do. This tree may seem too small to be pruned,
10   but to have the beautiful shape that I want it to have, it
11   needs to have its growth directed.
12   ANN: I wish somebody would direct my growth.
13   SUE: I don't think you're putting on *that* much weight, Ann.
14   ANN: I was thinking about my life, not my size.
15   SUE: Oh, sorry.
16   ANN: It seems like I've been going through some tough times
17   in my faith lately. Things don't turn out like I plan. Or
18   just when I think I've got a handle on something, I find
19   a verse in the Bible that causes me to deal with it all over
20   again.

1   SUE: It sounds like *you* are being pruned.

2   ANN: What do you mean?

3   SUE: As Christians, somebody is directing our growth —

4   God. He prunes us, shapes us and makes us how he wants

5   us to be. You see, the image that he fashions us after is

6   Jesus.

7   ANN: Well, it hurts to be pruned.

8   SUE: It always does, but it's for the best. We are stronger,

9   prettier, happier and more useful when God directs our

10   growth.

11   ANN: Sounds like it's just part of growing up and maturing

12   as a Christian.

13   SUE: It is. The Apostle Paul wrote, "Just as you have received

14   Christ Jesus as Lord, continue to live in him, rooted and

15   built up in him, strengthened in the faith as you were

16   taught . . ." [1] *(Looks at the tree.)* There, I'm done.

17   ANN: That really is a pretty tree.

18   SUE: Care for some coffee?

19   ANN: Sure. *(SUE exits and ANN calls after her.)* All you did was

20   pinch the ends to get the shape you wanted? *(To herself)*

21   I wonder how this pinching technique would work on

22   my husband's shape.

23

24

25

26

27

28

29

30

31

32

33

34

35   [1] *Colossians 2:6, 7*

Bringing My World to God

THEME: **Friendship Evangelism** — If we are serious about bringing people to the Lord, then we must invest time in our friendships.

SCRIPTURE: **I Peter 3:15** — "Always be prepared to give an answer to everyone who asks you to give the reason for the hope that you have."

SYNOPSIS: In the game show "Bringing My World to God," contestants vote on the best way to lead their neighbors to the Lord. The point is made that if you have the concern for someone, then you are the best person to reach them.

CHARACTERS: Bob Host — the game show host, overly excited, too big for life.
Audrey Winston — sophisticated New York type.
Frank Speaking — a down-home kind of guy, always laughing.

COSTUMES: Suit and tie for Bob Host, regular attire for contestants.

PROPS: None.

SOUND EFFECTS: Game show-type music, buzzer.

SETTING: The set of a game show. Place a podium or music stand Center Stage for the host and a table off to one side for the two contestants to stand or sit behind.

"Well, Bob, I have to say this is a tough question . . ."

1   *(Scene opens with all three actors already On-stage. While the*
2   *music is playing, the contestants should be talking animatedly*
3   *with BOB. As music fades, they take their places.)*
4   **BOB: Hi! I'm your host, Bob Host, and welcome to "Bringing**
5   **My World to God." This is the award-losing game show**
6   **where each week we try to guess what is the best way to**
7   **bring a certain segment of our society to God. This week**
8   **we will be challenging our contestants to guess the most**
9   **effective method of reaching our *neighbors*. Our**
10   **contestants are Audrey Winston . . .**
11   **AUDREY: Hello.**
12   **BOB: . . . and Frank Speaking.**
13   **FRANK: Howdy!**
14   **BOB: Let's begin, shall we? Contestants, the first situation is,**
15   **"You are hoping to introduce your neighbors to God, but**
16   **you have never talked together about spiritual things**
17   **before." What is the best first step? Number one — invite**
18   **them to go to a huge evangelistic crusade at _____**
19   **Stadium.** *(Insert the name of your nearest stadium or*
20   *auditorium.)* **Number two — invite them for coffee in a**

1   nonthreatening situation. Or number three — invite
2   them to a Casino Night at your church.
3   AUDREY: Excuse me, Bob, but would the pastor give a bit of
4   a testimony at the Casino Night?
5   BOB: I don't think so, Audrey. Frank, let's start with you.
6   What do you think is the best first step?
7   FRANK: Well, Bob, I have to say this is a hard question,
8   'cause in the ten years I've been a Christian, I've never
9   known anyone I wanted to invite anywhere. But, I pick
10   number one. It seems like a crusade would be a good
11   place to start.
12   BOB: Audrey, what is your vote?
13   AUDREY: Hmmm . . . if the pastor were to say something at
14   the Casino Night, then that would get my vote. Otherwise,
15   I think Frank is right. The crusade would be the thing
16   to invite them to. *(Buzzer)*
17   BOB: I'm sorry. The correct answer is number two — invite
18   them for coffee in a nonthreatening situation. The vast
19   majority of people who become Christians do so in the
20   context of a one-on-one conversation with someone they
21   already have a friendship with. *(AUDREY and FRANK*
22   *look very surprised.)* OK. Situation number two: "Your
23   neighbor tells you that you are the only Christian she
24   knows. She says she would like to ask you some questions
25   about spiritual things." Do you, one — invite her to
26   church on Sunday so she can meet the pastor? Two —
27   give her Billy Graham's address? Or three — talk to her
28   yourself? Audrey, let's start with you.
29   AUDREY: To have her write Billy Graham gets my vote. Billy
30   answers those kinds of questions all the time.
31   BOB: How about you, Frank?
32   FRANK: I disagree with Audrey. I think this neighbor gal
33   wants to talk *now*. She won't want to wait until Mr.
34   Graham has time to write her back. I say bring her to
35   church and let the pastor talk to her. That's what we pay

1   **the pastor for.** *(Buzzer)*

2 **BOB:** **Oh, boy. You're both wrong again. The answer is —**

3   **talk to her yourself. After all, you are the one person she**

4   **knows, so she will feel the most comfortable talking with**

5   **you.** *(AUDREY and FRANK ad-lib sounds of disbelief and*

6   *disparging remarks.)* **Contestants, we are running out of**

7   **time. This will be the lightning round. The last question**

8   **is, "If you want your neighbors to know God, then who**

9   **should be responsible to pray for them?" Number one —**

10   **you. Number two — you. Or number three — you. Frank,**

11   **let's have you lead on this one.** *(Each "you" should have a*

12   *different inflection on it. When the contestants respond, their*

13   *inflection should match that of the host's on that particular*

14   *number "you.")*

15 **FRANK:** **Whoa, Bob, you've saved the hardest for last!**

16   *(Grimaces.)* **I guess I'll have to say number three — you.**

17   *(FRANK points at BOB as he says this.)*

18 **BOB:** **You know, of course, Frank, that "you" means you,**

19   *(BOB points to FRANK)* **not "you," meaning me?**

20 **FRANK:** *(Confused)* **Uh, right — you, you.**

21 **BOB:** **How about you, Audrey?**

22 **FRANK:** **Audrey is a "you," too?** *(To himself)* **This is too hard!**

23 **AUDREY:** **I pick number one — you.**

24 **BOB:** **Audrey, you are absolutely right. The answer is**

25   **number one — you. This is because the Lord puts in our**

26   **hearts the people that he wants us to be concerned about.**

27   **Well, we're out of time. Audrey, it looks like you won this**

28   **round today on reaching our neighbors.** *(Turns toward the*

29   *congregation.)* **Remember, God wants *you* to reach your**

30   **neighbor for him. Tune in next week when we try to**

31   **discover the best way to bring unemployed steel workers**

32   **with navy tattoos to God.** *(Game show music comes back on.)*

33

34

35

The Choir Member

THEME: **The Christian Community** — Christians should go through life with the support and help of other believers.

SCRIPTURE: **I Corinthians 12:27** — "Now you are the body of Christ, and each one of you is a part of it."

Acts 2:42-47 — The early Christian community.

SYNOPSIS: Two friends meet in a music store and talk about their respective choirs. One is the only member of her choir. This absurdity is related to how people try to be "Lone Ranger" Christians.

CHARACTERS: Kathy
Julie
Narrator

COSTUMES: Regular attire.

PROPS: Music books.

SETTING: A music store. Place a table Center Stage to hold the music books.

"So, you really think I need to sing in a choir that has more than one person in it?"

1   **NARRATOR:**   **In the Bible, being a Christian is always talked**
2   **about in the context of the church — the Christian**
3   **community. God never meant for us to live the Christian**
4   **life on our own. To try and be a "Lone Ranger" Christian**
5   **is somewhat of a contradiction in terms — rather like the**
6   **choir member who was looking for music for her choir**
7   **one day . . .**
8   *(Scene opens with KATHY browsing in a music store. She is*
9   *picking up the books and looking at the list of tunes and humming*
10   *a few bars. It is not important whether or not KATHY can carry*
11   *a tune.)*
12   **KATHY:** *(Looking at a book)* **This would be a great song to do . . .**
13   *(She starts singing a few bars of a popular religious song*
14   *hopelessly off key.)*
15   **JULIE:** *(Walks On-stage, stops and peers at KATHY.)* **Hey, Kathy?**
16   **Hi, how are you doing?**
17   **KATHY:**   **Great! Julie, right? I met you at a Campus Crusade**
18   **for Choir rally.**
19   **JULIE:**   **That's right. So, what are you doing here?**
20   **KATHY:**   **I'm actually looking for choir music. I came away**

1   from that rally so inspired that I decided to become a
2   choir member.
3   JULIE: So you gave your life to choir. That's wonderful.
4   KATHY: Yup, it's pretty exciting. Being a choir member has
5   changed my life.
6   JULIE: *(Laughs.)* It's supposed to. So what local choir did you
7   join?
8   KATHY: Pardon me?
9   JULIE: What choir are you singing with?
10 KATHY: *(Looks around somewhat mystified.)* I sing by myself.
11 JULIE: Kathy, you can't be a choir member without a choir.
12 KATHY: I can't? Why not?
13 JULIE: Because by definition, being a choir member means
14   you are a part of a choir, and you need other choir
15   members to have a choir.
16 KATHY: But it seems to be working quite well. I don't have
17   any trouble scheduling rehearsals, and there haven't
18   been any disagreements over which songs to sing . . .
19 JULIE: *(Picking up on KATHY's comments)* . . . and no one to
20   tell you that you are singing flat. Sure, it's *easier*, but it's
21   not *better*. You see, there is also no one to hold you
22   accountable and to make sure that your singing is getting
23   better. The world sings very flat. It can be hard not to be
24   influenced by its terrible sense of pitch. You could lose
25   the tune altogether unless you are a part of a good choir.
26 KATHY: So, you really think I need to sing in a choir that has
27   more than one person in it?
28 JULIE: I do. Why don't you come and check out the choir that
29   I sing in? We'd like to teach the world to sing in perfect
30   harmony. I think you'll feel right at home. *(Freeze)*
31 NARRATOR: Scripture tells us that all Christians are a part
32   of the body of Christ. Are you a choir member without a
33   choir?
34
35

Christianity Lite

THEME: **Commitment** — Sometimes our faith is a reflection of the shallowness of our culture.

SCRIPTURE: **Ephesians 4:17-24** — "Put off your old self, which is being corrupted by its deceitful desires . . . and put on the new self, created to be like God . . ."

SYNOPSIS: A man gives a "pitch" for Christianity Lite, a version of the faith that has 1/10th of the commitment but all the promises. This sketch is a parody of a soft drink commercial.

CHARACTERS: Tennis celebrity — male or female.

COSTUMES: Shirt, shorts, tennis shoes.

PROPS: Pop can with "Christianity Lite" label, tennis racket.

SETTING: A TV commercial set.

"That's why I was so excited when I found this: New 'Christianity Lite.' "

1   *(Scene opens with the celebrity finishing a game of tennis. He/she*
2   *wipes his/her brow and begins to speak.)*
3   **TENNIS CELEBRITY:** **Hey, if you're like me, after a long**
4   **game of tennis or a tough day at work, the last thing you**
5   **need is regular Christianity with all its moral obligations**
6   **and commitments. I've always liked the taste and**
7   **appearance of regular Christianity, but for me and my**
8   **lifestyle, it's just too sweet. That's why I was so excited**
9   **when I found this:** *(Holding up pop can)* **New "Christianity**
10   **Lite" with Nutrasweet. It's a faith that has all the same**
11   **promises and the same appearance of the old**
12   **Christianity, but only a tenth of the commitment. Now I**
13   **don't have to be concerned if I never spend time in prayer**
14   **or Bible reading, or if I never help a neighbor in need.**
15   **That's all behind me now. Hey, if you like being a**
16   **Christian but find that it gets in the way of how you want**
17   **to live your life, then I recommend this: "Christianity**
18   **Lite." The faith for the "me" kind of person.**
19
20

The Christian Plant

THEME: **Growth** — As Christians, we are called to grow. We need to take care of our spiritual health.

SCRIPTURE: **II Timothy 3:14-17** — "Continue in what you have learned . . . from infancy you have known the holy Scriptures, which are able to make you wise for Salvation through faith in Christ Jesus."

SYNOPSIS: Two people bring in their Christian plants to the doctor. One is in great shape and one is dying from neglect.

CHARACTERS: Becky
Robin

COSTUMES: Regular attire.

PROPS: Two plants of the same kind: one is very healthy and one is obviously not.

SETTING: The waiting room of the plant doctor. Place several chairs Center Stage.

"Look, how can you expect this plant to grow if you don't feed it?"

1 (Scene opens with ROBIN sitting in a chair with a gorgeous
2 plant in her lap. She should be humming contentedly and
3 occasionally gaze lovingly at the plant. BECKY enters looking
4 worried and downcast.)
5 **BECKY:** Are you here to see the doctor too?
6 **ROBIN:** Yes. I just brought my plant in for its annual check
7 up. What's wrong with your plant? It doesn't look so well.
8 **BECKY:** I think it's dying but I don't know why, so I've
9 brought it in to see Dr. _____. (Insert last name of your
10 pastor.) I'm hoping he'll be able to help.
11 **ROBIN:** Oooh . . .
12 **BECKY:** Say, what kind of plant do you have? It's so lush and
13 healthy looking.
14 **ROBIN:** Oh, this is a "Christian plant."
15 **BECKY:** A Christian plant! That's what my plant is!
16 **ROBIN:** That's a Christian plant? It looks terrible. What on
17 earth have you been feeding it?
18 **BECKY:** Feeding it?
19 **ROBIN:** Yes, what kind of food have you been giving it?
20 **BECKY:** Food?

1   ROBIN: You mean you haven't been giving it anything to eat?
2   BECKY: Like what?
3   ROBIN: Well, does it get regular worship?
4   BECKY: Well, no, but sometimes I leave the Christian radio
5   station on when I go out.
6   ROBIN: Hmmm. That soil looks pretty bad. Is it rooted in the
7   Word?
8   BECKY: That it is! There is ground-up newspaper in this soil!
9   ROBIN: No, I mean the Word of God . . . the *Bible*. Look, how
10   can you expect this plant to grow and be healthy if you
11   don't feed it anything?
12 BECKY: I don't know. I guess I thought it would automatically
13   grow just because it *is* a Christian plant. What do you think
14   I should do? Or do you think it's hopeless?
15 ROBIN: Hey, with God, nothing is hopeless. I'd start out with
16   *mega* doses of vitamin B for Bible, vitamin C for
17   commitment and vitamin D for discipleship. Then sprinkle
18   with or "immerse in" living water and make sure it
19   participates in worship regularly to get good air from the
20   winds of the Spirit. Most importantly, remember to feed it
21   *daily* so that it becomes rooted in the Word.
22 BECKY: Wow! You sound like you really know what you're
23   talking about.
24 ROBIN: Well, my plant hasn't always been this healthy.
25 BECKY: Hey, thanks a lot. Now I know how to help this plant
26   become healthy. *(Stands up to leave.)* Say, do you know
27   anything about teenager plants?
28
29
30
31
32
33
34
35

Counting the Cost

THEME: **Discipleship** — As Christians, we need to be able to see the big picture of discipleship, count the cost, and be prepared to pay that cost.

SCRIPTURE: **Luke 14:28-30** — "Suppose one of you wants to build a tower. Will he not first sit down and estimate the cost to see if he has enough money to complete it?"

SYNOPSIS: A man who runs a construction company orders from minute to minute without looking ahead and preparing accordingly. His pastor helps him to see that the frustration in his spiritual life comes from the same lack of preparation.

CHARACTERS: Chuck — construction superintendent
Bob — Chuck's pastor
Alice — Chuck's secretary, a rather dizzy type

COSTUMES: Hard hat for Chuck.

PROPS: A note pad and anything that might give the impression of a disheveled office.

SETTING: The office of a construction company. Put a desk Center Stage with a disorganized array of papers on top.

"It's taking forever to get this building put up!"

1 *(Scene opens with CHUCK sitting at his desk giving instructions*
2 *to ALICE.)*
3 **CHUCK: How many cement blocks do they need to do**
4 **another row on all four walls?**
5 **ALICE: I *believe* the foreman said one hundred and thirty-four.**
6 **CHUCK: Then let's order another one hundred and thirty-**
7 **four and tell the yard to get them here fast. I don't want**
8 **the men standing around.**
9 **ALICE: Yes, sir. On the money, sir.** *(She exits.)*
10 **CHUCK:** *(Frustrated)* **It's taking forever to get this building**
11 **put up. It seems like I'm constantly ordering cement**
12 **blocks!**
13 **BOB:** *(Knocking)* **Hello!**
14 **CHUCK:** *(Absorbed in plans on his desk)* **C'mon in.** *(BOB enters.*
15 *CHUCK looks up.)* **Oh, hi, Pastor.**
16 **BOB: Hi, Chuck. I was in the area, so I thought I'd stop by and**
17 **see how you were doing.**
18 **CHUCK: Well, to be honest, I've been rather frustrated lately.**
19 **BOB: Maybe . . .** *(ALICE enters and interrupts BOB.)*
20 **ALICE: Sir, the men need more cement blocks.**

1   CHUCK: But I just had you order more.

2   ALICE: I *believe* they have already used them, sir.

3   CHUCK: OK, OK, order another one hundred and thirty-four.

4   ALICE: Yes, sir. On the money, sir. *(She exits.)*

5   CHUCK: I just never seem to be on top of things in my spiritual

6   life. It seems like I'm never quite ready for what's coming

7   next. It's like I just react to what happens.

8   BOB: Well, there is really no way to know what God is going

9   to allow to happen next, but as believers, we must lead a

10   life of preparation.

11   CHUCK: How do we do that?

12   BOB: One of the ways is to not just live minute to minute, but

13   to think about our faith in the context of a lifetime. Start

14   making decisions how that can support following Jesus

15   for the rest of your life.

16   CHUCK: It sounds like you're talking about seeing the big

17   picture and not just trying to jump the hurdle right in

18   front of us.

19   BOB: That's right. In fact . . . *(ALICE enters and interrupts.)*

20   ALICE: Sir, you wife just called to remind you to make the

21   monthly payment on your new Ford pick-up.

22   CHUCK: I paid that last month.

23   ALICE: Sir, I *believe* that you pay every month for another

24   fifty-nine months. I *believe* you signed a sixty-month

25   payment plan.

26   CHUCK: *(Aghast)* I did? I don't have that kind of money! I

27   thought I just had to pay one time. *(To himself)* Three

28   hundred and fifteen dollars did seem like a pretty good

29   price for a brand new truck, especially when they gave me

30   a fifteen-hundred-dollar rebate. OK, pay it.

31   ALICE: Yes, sir. On the money, sir. Oh, and sir?

32   CHUCK: Yes, Alice?

33   ALICE: The men need more cement blocks. They've used all

34   that we have ordered.

35   CHUCK: Order enough for another row then. Get one

1   hundred thirty-four more.

2   ALICE: Excuse me, sir, but are we planning on finishing this

3   building?

4   CHUCK: Of course we are.

5   ALICE: Then that means we will need another five rows of

6   cement blocks to finish all the walls.

7   CHUCK: Yes, that would be right.

8   ALICE: Sir, instead of going row by row, why don't we order

9   enough blocks to finish the walls? That way we won't

10   need to be continually calling in orders, and the men

11   won't have to stand around on the site.

12 CHUCK: Alice, that's a great idea. Go ahead and take care

13   of it.

14 ALICE: Yes, sir. On the money, sir! *(She exits.)*

15 CHUCK: *(Wonderingly)* I never thought of looking at the

16   whole project and ordering enough blocks to finish the

17   job. I really can make decisions now that could make

18   things better later.

19 BOB: See Chuck, it's the same principle in your spiritual life

20   as well.

21 CHUCK: *(Not hearing)* This could make a big difference in how

22   I approach the new airport project in Denver. *(Or*

23   *substitute another big construction project in your area.)*

24 ALICE: *(Enters and interrupts again.)* Sir, the yard just called to

25   say that they have discontinued the line of cement blocks

26   we've been ordering. They are happy to send us their

27   new line of blocks. It's a little bigger and a different color.

28 CHUCK: It's definitely time to start counting the cost!

29 ALICE: Yes, sir. On the money, sir! *(Freeze)*

30

31

32

33

34

35

The Dream

THEME: **God's Omniscience** — The Lord knows all about us.

SCRIPTURE: **Psalm 139:1, 3** — "O Lord, you have searched me and you know me . . . you are familiar with all my ways."

SYNOPSIS: A fellow has a dream that everyone knows what he is thinking all the time. He awakens, relieved that only God, who is forgiving, knows him that well.

CHARACTERS: Off-stage voice of John
(Spoken into a microphone backstage.)
John
Store Clerk
Negative man
Lady in store

COSTUMES: Regular attire is fine. The clerk may wear a uniform if desired.

PROPS: None needed. The store merchandise may be pantomimed.

SETTING: A convenience store. Set a table off to one side of the of the stage for the clerk to stand behind.

1   *(Scene opens with CLERK behind counter and JOHN browsing*
2   *in the store.)*
3   **OFF-STAGE VOICE:** Last night I had a terrible dream! I
4   dreamt that everybody knew all about me and what I
5   was thinking. Let me tell you, it was scary . . .
6   **JOHN:** Let's see, I need to get a blue, medium Bic pen and a
7   Trident Sugarless cinnamon-flavored double pack of
8   gum.
9   **NEGATIVE MAN:** *(Enters.)* Well, if it isn't John. If you hadn't
10   looked on Marcia's paper during the test on Friday,
11   March 11th, 1983, you would have flunked for sure. You're
12   a cheat, John Smith!
13   **JOHN:** How do you know about that? That was over _____
14   *(Insert correct number of years)* **years ago!**
15   **NEGATIVE MAN:** Everybody knows all about you. Every-
16   body knows what you're thinking all the time!
17   **JOHN:** Hi. I'd like . . .
18   **STORE CLERK:** . . . a blue, medium Bic pen and a Trident
19   Sugarless cinnamon-flavored double pack of gum.
20   **JOHN:** *(In awe)* Uh, yeah. That's what I want.
21   **STORE CLERK:** Well, I'm not going to sell you anything.
22   Anybody who yells at his parents the way that you did
23   last night doesn't deserve the convenience of a
24   convenience store!
25   **JOHN:** I didn't mean to. I apologized . . . *(Backs into lady.)*
26   Excuse me, Ma'am.
27   **LADY:** Ha! You don't mean that. You were thinking, "Get out
28   of my way, you skinny lady!" Ha! Ha!
29   **JOHN:** No, no, someone help me . . . *(Freeze)*
30   **OFF-STAGE VOICE:** That's when I woke up. Thank goodness
31   it was just a dream. And thank goodness that the only
32   person who does know everything about me is my
33   heavenly Father, and he loves me and accepts me as I am.
34
35

Fat Jack

THEME: **Forgiveness** — The greater the debt forgiven, the greater the gratitude.

SCRIPTURE: **Luke 7:41-43** — The parable of the two debtors.

SYNOPSIS: An old man reminisces about how he learned of forgiveness in a casino he once owned.

CHARACTERS: Old Fat Jack — skinny older guy
Young Fat Jack — skinny younger guy
Knuckles — tough guy
Loser One
Loser Two
Bookkeeper

COSTUMES: Old Fat Jack and Young Fat Jack can wear suits. Knuckles may wear a black leather jacket.

PROPS: People can be props or the actors can mime the slot machines, etc.

SETTING: Fat Jack's Casino. Set a desk off to one side of the stage for the Bookkeeper.

"Oh, please don't kill me, Mr. Fat."

1   *(Scene opens with OLD FAT JACK Downstage. Upstage, frozen*
2   *until his scene starts, is YOUNG FAT JACK playing a slot*
3   *machine. The slot machine can be a person with one arm bent*
4   *up like the arm of a machine. The BOOKKEEPER is sitting at*
5   *his desk.)*
6   **OLD FAT JACK:**   **How can God forgive someone like me?**
7   **Many of my old friends have asked that. They seem to**
8   **think that someone who has led a life as sinful as I have**
9   **is beyond God's reach. Well, let me tell you a story about**
10   **forgiveness. I used to own a casino, and they called me**
11   **Fat Jack . . .**
12   **YOUNG FAT JACK:**   **Hah, I feel lucky today!** *(Pulls down the*
13   *arm of the slot machine.)* **Not lucky enough, I guess. How**
14   **are we doing, Bookkeeper?**
15   **BOOKKEEPER:**   **You're doing great, Fat Jack. We're rolling**
16   **in the dough.**
17   **YOUNG FAT JACK:**   **That's great! Pretty soon I'll own this**
18   **whole town!**
19   **KNUCKLES:**   *(Enters holding LOSER ONE and LOSER TWO by*
20   *their collars.)* **Hey, boss . . .**

1   **YOUNG FAT JACK:** What have you got there, Knuckles?

2   **KNUCKLES:** These two guys lost bad at the tables and

3   couldn't pay up. I caught them trying to sneak out of the

4   casino.

5   **LOSER ONE:** Oh, please, Jack Spratt, don't kill me. I'll pay

6   you back. Honest, I will. I just don't have the money right

7   now, that's all.

8   **YOUNG FAT JACK:** The name is Fat Jack, not Jack Spratt.

9   **LOSER TWO:** Excuse me, Mr. Jack. If I might have a word

10   with you in private?

11   **YOUNG FAT JACK:** This is private. Say what's on your mind.

12   **LOSER TWO:** There appears to be an undue amount of

13   consternation over our seeming inability to rectify the

14   deficit in our substandard financial situation.

15   **YOUNG FAT JACK:** What is he saying?

16   **BOOKKEEPER:** He can't pay either.

17   **YOUNG FAT JACK:** How much do these folks owe me,

18   Knuckles?

19   **KNUCKLES:** He *(LOSER ONE)* owes you $175,000, and *he*

20   *(LOSER TWO)* owes you $25,000.

21   **LOSER ONE:** *(On his knees and hugging at JACK's leg)* Oh,

22   please don't kill me, Mr. Fat.

23   **LOSER TWO:** Listen, I have some property in Whittier,

24   California that you can have as a down payment on the

25   money I owe you.

26   **YOUNG FAT JACK:** No . . . No . . . Listen, I'm doing quite

27   well right now, and I remember when I was a no-good,

28   two-bit operator like you two. Let's just forget about the

29   money and call it even Steven.

30   **LOSER ONE:** Call it Steven?

31   **YOUNG FAT JACK:** Call it whatever you like, but you are free

32   to go.

33   **LOSER ONE:** Free to go?

34   **KNUCKLES:** *(Hauls LOSER ONE to his feet.)* **Hit the road,**

35   **Jack!** *(FAT JACK looks at him threateningly.)* **That's a figure**

1   of speech, Jack.

2   **LOSER ONE:**   Thank you so much! *(Kisses hand of JACK.)*

3   **LOSER TWO:** I would like to say that I am deeply

4   appreciative of this philanthropic gesture on your part.

5   **YOUNG FAT JACK:** You're pushing your luck, guys . . .

6   **LOSER TWO:** *(As he leaves)* Say . . . would you be interested

7   in *buying* my property in Whittier? *(Freeze)*

8   **OLD FAT JACK:**   So, I forgave those two losers of their debt.

9   The one who owed the greater debt was, of course, the

10   more grateful of the two. I think I got Christmas cards

11   from him for about five years after that. The point is,

12   although the money meant a lot to them, I was wealthy.

13   The $200,000 was not important to me. How does that

14   relate to my forgiveness? When I finally gave my life to

15   the Lord, I thought, "Hey, Fat Jack, you've done a lot of

16   wrong that you're gonna have to pay for." But he forgave

17   me. It turned out that just like my account could cover

18   the $200,000, he could cover my sin. He has more than

19   enough forgiveness for all the sins of the world combined,

20   and he proved that once already.

21

22

23

24

25

26

27

28

29

30

31

32

33

34

35

The Fishermen

THEME: **Evangelism** — We need to do more than just talk about sharing our beliefs with others; we need to get out and "just do it."

SCRIPTURE: **Matthew 4:19, Mark 1:17, Matthew 28:19** — "I will make you fishers of men."

SYNOPSIS: Two people who claim to be fishermen bump into each other. In the ensuing discussion, it becomes apparent that one has all the gear but never actually gets out and fishes, while the other catches fish all the time with little gear at all.

CHARACTERS: Bob
Dan
(Fishing buddies; could be Sarah and Beth)
Narrator

COSTUMES: Bob should be dressed in old jeans and a shirt — nothing fancy. Dan, on the other hand, should be decked out in serious fisherman's gear: fishing vest and hat (with assorted flies stuck in the hat and vest), creel, boots, etc.

PROPS: A cane fishing pole baited with a worm hook, and elaborate fishing gear (e.g. huge tackle box, two or three fishing poles, lots of lures, spinning tackle, open-faced reel, a couple of nets, etc.).

SETTING: The great outdoors.

"But Dan, the whole point of fishing is getting out there and catching fish."

1	*(Scene opens with BOB standing On-stage, whistling a tune. He*
2	*is holding his simple cane fishing pole. DAN enters laden down*
3	*with all kinds of fancy fishing gear.)*
4	**BOB: Dan? Well I'll be, Dan Winker. I haven't seen you in**
5	**ages!**
6	**DAN: Bob, how's it going?**
7	**BOB: Great. How have you been?**
8	**DAN: Oh fine, fine. It looks like you've been doing some**
9	**fishing.**
10	**BOB: Yeah, I was up the _____ *(Name of local river***
11	***or lake)* this morning. I caught a couple of pan-sized trout.**
12	**How about you?**
13	**DAN: Humph. Well, I've just come back from a trip myself. I**
14	**did pretty well too. When you've got gear as good as I**
15	**have, you want to get out as often as you can.**
16	**BOB: I guess so. So how many did you catch?**
17	**DAN: Well, I uh, actually I didn't keep any of them, so I lost**
18	**track. I always throw them back. I don't like to eat fish,**
19	**you know.**
20	**BOB: Oh. So where did you go fishing?**

1   DAN: *(Hotly)* **Why does it matter where I went and if I**
2   **caught anything? I've got all this great gear so that makes**
3   **me a fisherman, right?**
4   BOB: **What are you talking about, Dan? Catching fish makes**
5   **you a fisherman — not the equipment you have.**
6   *(Suspiciously)* **Say, your boots look awfully clean to have**
7   **been up in the woods this morning.**
8   DAN: **Well — well actually I was just at a friend's house this**
9   **morning watching a video on fishing. But if I *had* been**
10   **out somewhere, I know I would've caught a fish. I've read**
11   **all kinds of fishing books, I've taken classes on fishing,**
12   **and I've even tied and sold some of my own flies!**
13   BOB: **But you don't actually get out into the woods and *go***
14   **fishing?**
15   DAN: **Well no, not really. I don't like to clean fish, and this**
16   **equipment is so nice that I hate to get it dirty.**
17   BOB: **But, Dan, the whole point of fishing is getting out there**
18   **and catching fish. You're so busy looking like a fisherman**
19   **and studying fishing that you never get out and actually**
20   **do it.**
21   DAN: **That may be true, but someday I'm going to get out and**
22   **fish and when I do, watch out!**
23   NARRATOR: **Jesus said, "I will make you fishers of men."** [1]
24   **Are we like Bob, actively out there fishing day after day,**
25   **or are we like Dan, busying ourselves with books, talks,**
26   **and seminars on how to fish but never actually getting**
27   **out there and doing it?**
28
29
30
31
32
33
34
35   [1] *Matthew 4:19*

Forever Life Insurance

THEME: **Eternal Life, Salvation.**

SCRIPTURE: **John 3:16** — "For God so loved the world that he gave his one and only Son, that whoever believes in him shall not perish but have eternal life."

SYNOPSIS: An old man tries to buy eternal life insurance and finds that it is impossible to purchase salvation.

CHARACTERS: Woman — Salesperson
Man — Elderly gentleman buying insurance

COSTUMES: Businesslike attire for the woman.

PROPS: Papers and pens.

SETTING: The office of an insurance company. Set a desk or small table and chair Center Stage. Place a telephone on the desk.

1 *(Scene opens with WOMAN sitting at the desk, working on papers*
2 *or ad-libbing talking on the phone. MAN enters.)*
3 MAN: *(Brashly)* **I'm looking to buy some eternal life insurance.**
4 **I found out my Social Security** *(Or Canada Pension)* **is only**
5 **good until I die, so I need some coverage for after "then."**
6 WOMAN: **Well, sir, you've certainly come to the right place.**
7 **We here at "Forever Life Insurance" pride ourselves on**
8 **having a variety of policies to suit any price range.**
9 MAN: **Well, price is no object. I'm eighty-five years old, and I've**
10 **worked hard to have a comfortable retirement. And now**
11 **that the time is close when I'll be moving on to** *(Licks lips)*
12 **... another life. I want to make sure I've got good coverage**
13 **so I end up at the right place, if you know what I mean.**
14 *(Laughs.)* **So, if it means selling some of my stocks,**
15 *(Condominiums, farms, sailboats, etc.)* **I'll do it. What have you**
16 **got?**
17 WOMAN: *(Shuffles through her papers and pulls one out.)* **This one**
18 **is our generic policy, so it's also our cheapest. It's your**
19 **basic "Fire Insurance," and it's designed to protect you**
20 **from the "other place."**
21 MAN: *(Interrupting)* **Naw, that sounds too cheap. I've never died**
22 **before, and frankly, I think I might need better insurance**
23 **than that. I haven't always been as nice and easygoing as**
24 **I am now.** *(Laughs harshly.)* **What else have you got there?**
25 WOMAN: **Ahhh ...** *(Looking through papers)* **let's see ... we have**
26 **our "Forever Safe Policy." You buy in young and do**
27 **whatever you want the rest of your life until you die. But**
28 **that wouldn't apply to you. You're too old. Let's see here ...**
29 *(Shuffles more papers.)*
30 MAN: *(Aside — to himself)* **Yeah, I guess you could say that I've**
31 **been more concerned about my earthly old age than my**
32 **"eternal forever."** *(Looks up toward the ceiling pensively.)*
33 WOMAN: *(Enthusiastically)* **Ah, here we have it. Our "Jesus**
34 **Early Warning" policy. It is supposed to warn you just**
35 **before Jesus comes, so you can —**

1   **MAN:** *(Interrupting)* **No, I still could die before Jesus comes**
2   **back. Don't you have anything like a "Good Life" policy?**
3   **You know, like you get to go to heaven because you lived**
4   **a good life, didn't kick dogs, things like that?**
5   **WOMAN:**   **Well, we used to offer that policy, but we couldn't**
6   **guarantee it, so we quit selling it.**
7   **MAN:**   **Well, what policy** *can* **you guarantee then?**
8   **WOMAN:**   **Our "Eternal Life Policy." But it's expensive.**
9   **MAN:**   **I didn't hoard, save, and invest all my money all my life**
10   **for nothing. How much? Ten thousand dollars? Fifty**
11   **thousand dollars?** *(WOMAN shakes her head "no" as he names*
12   *figures.)* **One hundred thousand dollars?** *(He becomes irate.)*
13   **Well, what does it cost then?**
14   **WOMAN:**   **Your heart.**
15   **MAN:**   *(Surprised)* **My heart?** *(Scratches his head.)* **Boy, that** *is*
16   **expensive! That's your last policy, eh?**
17   **WOMAN:**   **Yes, sir. It may cost the most, but it's also the best.**
18   **MAN:**   *(Getting up)* **Well, that's a pretty steep price. I'd better**
19   **shop around. There may be a better deal somewhere else,**
20   **and I'm sure I saw an ad in the paper for a "Good Life"**
21   **policy.** *(To himself)* **And it said they were giving five free**
22   **tanning sessions to the first ten customers. I'd better**
23   **hurry.** *(Freeze)*
24
25
26
27
28
29
30
31
32
33
34
35

Grading on the Curve

THEME: **Judgment** — A man reaps what he sows.

SCRIPTURE: **Galatians 6:7** — "Do not be deceived: God cannot be mocked. A man reaps what he sows."

SYNOPSIS: Two students talking about an exam find out that their approach to their studies yields vastly different results. Likewise, our way of living can produce good or bad results.

CHARACTERS: Lindsey — a high school student who does as little as possible to pass her classes
Rene — a hardworking, straight A student
Narrator

COSTUMES: Regular attire.

PROPS: Each student should have an armful of books.

SETTING: School.

"If it hadn't been for you, I'd have a C instead of a D."

1   **NARRATOR:**   **In Scripture it says, "Do not be deceived: God**
2   **cannot be mocked. A man reaps what he sows."** [1] **That's**
3   **rather like the two girls who took a history exam.**
4   *(Scene opens with LINDSEY and RENE walking down the aisle*
5   *toward the stage talking.)*
6   **LINDSEY:**   **That was such a dumb history test! I'm glad I had**
7   **that gum wrapper with the dates written on it with me.**
8   **RENE:**   *(Stopping)* **You cheated on that test?**
9   **LINDSEY:**   **I** *had* **to! Mr. Glanzer asked such dumb questions.**
10   **Besides, it's a good thing I did. I only passed that test by**
11   **one point! I would've been OK but somebody got ninety-**
12   **eight percent and ruined the curve!**
13   **RENE:**   *(Starting to walk again)* **Oh . . .**
14   **LINDSEY:**   **How did you do, Rene?**
15   **RENE:**   **OK, I guess.**
16   **LINDSEY:**   **It was a dumb test. What exactly did you get?**
17   **RENE:**   **Ninety-eight percent.**
18   **LINDSEY:**   **Ninety-eight percent. If it hadn't been for you, I**
19   **would have a C instead of a D. How am I going to pass**
20   [1] *Galatians 6:7*

1   my classes if you're taking all the same tests that I am?

2 RENE: Lindsey . . . listen to yourself. You want to pass your

3   classes but you don't want to study or learn anything.

4 LINDSEY: Hey, I studied for my history class. I watched *Back*

5   *to the Future I* and *II*. *(To herself)* I think that was history . . .

6 RENE: You can't expect to get the grades you want if you're

7   not willing to do the work.

8 LINDSEY: I don't think Mr. Glanzer would fail me, he likes

9   me. Besides, my dad is on the school board.

10 RENE: Don't kid yourself — you can't fool Mr. Glanzer. He

11   knows whether or not you know the material.

12 LINDSEY: You're starting to sound like my mom!

13 RENE: Well, I always thought your mom was pretty smart.

14 LINDSEY: *(Reluctantly)* I guess what you're saying makes

15   sense, Rene. In fact, I could still get some studying done

16   before our chemistry test next class.

17 RENE: Oh no! I completely forgot about that! I never studied!

18 LINDSEY: You didn't? Great! I can pass this one without

19   studying!

20

21

22

23

24

25

26

27

28

29

30

31

32

33

34

35

The Greatest Bowl Game of All — Life

THEME: **Discipline** — To live as God calls us to live requires spiritual discipline. To grow and develop as believers means we must exercise daily, much as an athlete does.

SCRIPTURE: **I Corinthians 9:24** — "Run in such a way as to get the prize."
I Timothy 4:8 — "For physical training is of some value, but godliness has value for all things . . ."
Hebrews 12:1 — "Let us run with perseverance the race marked out for us."
Philippians 4:13 — "I can do everything through him who gives me strength."

SYNOPSIS: In three vignettes which can be done back to back or sprinkled throughout the service, Commentator Joel Fay gives us tips on how to be prepared for The Greatest Bowl Game of All — Life. Behind him as he speaks are different plays from football, re-enacted to lend weight to his words.

CHARACTERS: Joel Fay — TV Commentator
Two or more football players — Linemen or linewomen. One should be small and the other should be large in comparison.

COSTUMES: Football helmets and pads, if available.

PROPS: Football, Bible.

SETTING: A football field.

"You, too, can be a better player in The Greatest Bowl Game of All — Life."

1　*(All three vignettes open the same way. The FOOTBALL*
2　*PLAYER(S) should silently pantomime the action while JOEL*
3　*walks into the corner of the picture. Although the FOOTBALL*
4　*PLAYERS are to mime their actions, a balance should be sought*
5　*to ensure the grimaces and movements do not upstage JOEL.*
6　*Scene opens with the two FOOTBALL PLAYERS down into*
7　*postion, making faces at each other across the line.)*
8　**JOEL:　Hello. I am Joel Fay speaking to you live from the**
9　**sidelines of The Greatest Bowl Game of All — Life! And**
10　**today I have some timely tips on how you, too, can be**
11　**better players in this game of life.**
12
13　**Vignette 1**
14　*(Off-stage someone yells "Hut." As JOEL speaks, the two*
15　*FOOTBALL PLAYERS charge each other and, though one is*
16　*larger, they stay even as they push one another. As time goes on,*
17　*however, the little FOOTBALL PLAYER starts to lose. Be*
18　*creative on how the little FOOTBALL PLAYER tries to keep the*
19　*big FOOTBALL PLAYER from getting by. Timing is important*
20　*here. As soon as the FOOTBALL PLAYERS are up against each*

1   *other, JOEL should begin to talk again.)*

2   **JOEL:**   **Do you sometimes feel like you are up against**

3   **insurmountable obstacles in your life? Do you often think**

4   **that it's impossible to press on? Do life's problems loom**

5   **large and ugly, threatening to overcome you? If you seem**

6   **to be losing in the bowl game of life, then I recommend**

7   **that you pick up a copy of this:** *(Holds up a Bible.)* **The**

8   **Official Playbook of Life. This book has all the winning**

9   **plays, strategies and pointers that you'll ever need to**

10   **help you lay a strong foundation and to play a winning**

11   **game.** *(Looks at the two FOOTBALL PLAYERS and then back*

12   *to the audience.)* **For example, listen to these encouraging**

13   **words. "Who is it that overcomes the world? Only he who**

14   **believes that Jesus is the Son of God,"** [1] **and "I can do**

15   **everything through [Christ] who gives me strength."** [2] **Do**

16   **you want to play a winning game and not be on the**

17   **defensive all the time?** *(The little FOOTBALL PLAYER*

18   *should now start to lose ground.)* **Would you like to play the**

19   **game with a sense of confidence? Then get a copy of the**

20   **playbook. It will make all the difference in your game.**

21   **You, too, can be a better player in The Greatest Bowl**

22   **Game of All — Life.** *(He smiles and walks over to the little*

23   *FOOTBALL PLAYER and hands him the Bible. The little*

24   *FOOTBALL PLAYER keeps pushing and bit by bit begins to*

25   *move the larger FOOTBALL PLAYER back, then both freeze.)*

26

27   **Vignette 2**

28

29   *(One FOOTBALL PLAYER is running in place. He is actually*

30   *running up the side of the field, looking over his shoulder to*

31   *catch a pass. JOEL enters.)*

32   **JOEL:**   **Hello, Joel Fay again, with more tips for playing in The**

33   **Greatest Bowl Game of All — Life.** *(He smiles and looks at the*

34   [1] *I John 5:5*

35   [2] *Philippians 4:13*

1   *FOOTBALL PLAYERS.)* **This man is going out to catch a**
2   **pass. The quarterback has thrown the ball, and it's**
3   **coming this way. Look how fast this athlete runs. See**
4   **what great shape he's in? Playing the Bowl Game of Life**
5   **by the playbook is playing life how God wants it played,**
6   **and that takes endurance, training and exercise. Life can**
7   **be long and hard with many unexpected changes. To be**
8   **ready for anything means being prepared by exercising**
9   **daily. To get those muscles in shape, the playbook**
10   **recommends staying healthy by eating daily from God's**
11   **Word — things like angel food cake and vitamin B for**
12   **Bible — but stay away from deviled eggs. Regular**
13   **exercise like praying, sharing your faith and meeting**
14   **together with other teammates to talk about plays is also**
15   **very important.** *(Addresses the FOOTBALL PLAYER.)* **Do**
16   **you think you would be able to play as effectively if you**
17   **hadn't trained for the game?**
18 **FOOTBALL PLAYER:** *(Huffing and puffing, he is still running*
19   *and expecting the pass.)* **I would be in big trouble if I hadn't**
20   **prepared myself according to the playbook. You've got**
21   **to be in shape if you expect to play a godly, winning game!**
22   **It isn't easy, though. Sometimes I just don't feel like**
23   **reading God's Word or praying. Sometimes my muscles**
24   **scream that they have had enough and that they want**
25   **to sleep in on a Sunday when I should be at church**
26   **exercising with the rest of the team.**
27 **JOEL:** **Well, we'll let you get back to your game. It looks like**
28   **the football is finally getting to you. That certainly is a**
29   *long bomb.* **Remember, playing the game by the playbook**
30   **means daily preparation and exercise in the form of**
31   **prayer, Bible reading, sharing your faith and worship.**
32   **It takes discipline and you may hate to work out, but**
33   **you'll feel better for it. You need to be in shape to play**
34   **in The Greatest Bowl Game of All — Life!** *(As soon as JOEL*
35   *is finished talking, the FOOTBALL PLAYER reaches out to*

1   *catch the ball, which should be thrown lightly to him from Off-*
2   *stage, he catches it so that it hits him right in the face guard*
3   *and sticks in the helmet with the point right between his eyes.*
4   *He tries to shake the ball out, then freezes.)*
5
6   **Vignette 3**
7
8   *(One FOOTBALL PLAYER is running in place with the ball*
9   *tucked close to his body. He is going for a touchdown. He is*
10   *pursued by at least one other person. For variety, they could do*
11   *this scene in slow motion. Regardless of how many people are*
12   *chasing him, they should all have on different colored helmets,*
13   *so that it is intentionally confusing as to how many teams there*
14   *are and who is on what team. JOEL enters.)*
15 JOEL: **Hello. Joel Fay here one last time to talk to you about**
16   **the last few moments of The Greatest Bowl Game of All —**
17   **Life! If you played the game by the playbook and you**
18   **kept up your daily exercise so that the game didn't wear**
19   **you out, then you'll be able to run with endurance until**
20   **the finish is in sight. Yes, a touchdown is yours if you are**
21   **found true and committed to God at the end of the game.**
22   **This is where our bowl game differs a little from that of**
23   **the competition. There is only one touchdown per player**
24   **and it's always at the end of the game. So, anyway, train**
25   **daily and with determination. Read the playbook and**
26   **live by its plays. Run with perseverance the race set**
27   **before you.** *(He turns toward the FOOTBALL PLAYERS who*
28   *manage to catch up to the PLAYER with the ball. They all put*
29   *their hands on the football and move forward a little bit. At the*
30   *same time, the three FOOTBALL PLAYERS lift the ball into*
31   *the air and yell, "Touchdown!" Then continuing in slow motion,*
32   *they should jump up and give high fives and slap each other's*
33   *rear ends. Freeze.)*
34
35

The Great Physician

THEME: **Healing** — The church is like a hospital for hurt people.

SCRIPTURE: **Matthew 11:28** — "Come to me, all you who are weary and burdened, and I will give you rest."

SNYOPSIS: A patient in need of healing discovers the Great Physician is waiting to help him, anytime and anywhere.

CHARACTERS: Nurse
Patient

COSTUMES: Nurse's uniform, if desired.

PROPS: None.

SETTING: The waiting room of a doctor's office. A desk is needed for the nurse to sit at.

"I feel awful. My heart hurts so much . . . I think it may be broken."

1 (*Scene opens with NURSE at reception desk as PATIENT*
2 *enters.)*
3 **NURSE:** Can I help you?
4 **PATIENT:** Yes. I need to see the doctor, but I don't have an
5 appointment.
6 **NURSE:** Oh, that's OK. He has time for you.
7 **PATIENT:** He does?
8 **NURSE:** Sure, he has time for everyone. Now what seems to
9 be the problem?
10 **PATIENT:** Well, I feel awful. My heart hurts so much, I can
11 hardly move. I think it may be broken. I have bad family
12 problems and just yesterday I found out my payroll check
13 bounced. I don't think I can take it anymore.
14 **NURSE:** How long have you had this condition?
15 **PATIENT:** For quite a while now. I've been trying to take
16 care of it on my own, but now everything is getting out
17 of hand.
18 **NURSE:** Well, I'm confident that the doctor will be able to
19 help you. After all, he *is* the Great Physician.
20 **PATIENT:** I heard about him. Doesn't he have other offices too?

1   NURSE: All over town.

2   PATIENT: And he gets to all the offices?

3   NURSE: Well, actually he is at all the offices, all over town,

4   all the time! Plus, he is out there, too! *(Motions toward the*

5   *outside.)*

6   PATIENT: Wow! What does he call his business?

7   NURSE: He calls it "church." The Great Physician has set up

8   offices all over so that people can get the healing they

9   need. It's kind of like a franchise.

10   PATIENT: Does he have a motto?

11   NURSE: He sure does. It's "Come to me, all you who are

12   weary and burdened, and I will give you rest . . . learn

13   from me, for I am gentle and humble in heart, and you

14   will find rest for your souls." [1]

15   PATIENT: *(Sigh)* That is exactly what I'm looking for. The

16   sooner I can see him, the better! But are all these patients

17   ahead of me? *(Should do a wave motion to indicate the*

18   *congregation.)*

19   NURSE: Don't worry, Ma'am/sir. The Great Physician can

20   see you all at the same time. *(Freeze)*

21

22

23

24

25

26

27

28

29

30

31

32

33

34

35   [1] *Matthew 11:28,29*

65

The Guide

THEME: **The Holy Spirit** — The Spirit acts as a guide in our lives.

SCRIPTURE: **John 14:26** — "But the Counselor, the Holy Spirit, whom the Father will send in my name, will teach you all things and will remind you of everything I have said to you."

SYNOPSIS: A city fella is on a hike in the mountains and finds out he should have a guide. Likewise, we also need a guide in our lives: the Holy Spirit.

CHARACTERS: Carl Spotrun — old mountain guide
John Q. Public — city fella
Narrator

COSTUMES: Flannel shirt, jeans, hiking boots for Carl Spotrun, suit for John Q. Public.

PROPS: Pocket knife, stick (to whittle on), briefcase.

SETTING: The mountains. Place a stool Center Stage for Carl to sit on as he whittles.

1   *(Scene opens with CARL whistling and whittling away on a*
2   *stick. JOHN comes huffing and puffing onto the stage.)*
3   **CARL: Hello there, young fella.**
4   **JOHN:** *(Huffing and puffing)* **Hi, old timer.** *(Puts down his*
5   *briefcase and stretches.)* **Boy, the mountains are sure steep**
6   **around here.**
7   **CARL: Yup, they sure are. Why don't you sit down a spell**
8   **and rest?**
9   **JOHN: Thanks, I think I will.** *(They sit for a beat or two, looking*
10   *out over the valley.)*
11   **CARL: What's your name, son?**
12   **JOHN: John Q. Public.**
13   **CARL: Say . . . I've heard of you. You're famous. Aren't you**
14   **the guy with 2.4 children?**
15   **JOHN: Yes, sir. That's me. What's your name?**
16   **CARL: My name is Carl Spotrun, but my friends just call me**
17   **"C."**
18   **JOHN:** *(Doesn't get it.)* **Hmmm . . . C. Spotrun. You look in great**
19   **shape, C. How old are you?**
20   **CARL: Well, John, I'm seventy-one years old. I'd be seventy-**
21   **three, but I was sick for two years. So, what brings you**
22   **into these parts?** *(Looks him up and down.)* **Are you an**
23   **insurance salesman?**
24   **JOHN: No sir, I'm on my first mountain vacation.**
25   **CARL: Going alone?**
26   **JOHN: Yes, sir.**
27   **CARL: Have you ever been in these mountains before?**
28   **JOHN: No. Not at all.**
29   **CARL: Maybe you should hire me as your guide.**
30   **JOHN: A guide? What do I need a guide for?**
31   **CARL: Well, I can help you find the nicest and prettiest spots**
32   **on the mountain. You could walk right by them and not**
33   **even know it!**
34   **JOHN: Oh, I hadn't thought of that.**
35   **CARL: Yup. I know these mountains and valleys like the**

1   back of my foot. I know the trails and what's coming
2   around the next corner. I could save you a lot of
3   frustration and worry.

4 JOHN: I hadn't thought of that either. When I decided to go
5   on a vacation in the mountains, I never stopped to think
6   that having a guide could make it more enjoyable!

7 CARL: I guarantee I can help you get the most out of your
8   vacation.

9 JOHN: Sounds great!

10 CARL: I should tell you, though, that some of the trails will
11   be hard. But if I'm your guide, I'll never take you on a
12   path that's too tough. Now if you go on your own, there's
13   no telling where you might end up. *(Gives JOHN a hard
14   look; JOHN shivers.)* That's why it's good to have a guide.

15 JOHN: I'm sold, C. You're hired. Is there anything special
16   I'll need?

17 CARL: Not really, although maybe you should get a beltfor.

18 JOHN: Yeah? What's a beltfor?

19 CARL: Usually to keep your pants up. *(Freeze)*

20 NARRATOR: Just as John needed a guide to make his trip
21   better, so we need the Holy Spirit to be our guide through
22   this journey of life.

23

24

25

26

27

28

29

30

31

32

33

34

35

The Health Club

THEME: **Growth** — As believers, we should be out and involved in everyday life, exercising our faith.

SCRIPTURE: **James 2:17** — "Faith by itself, if it is not accompanied by action, is dead."
James 1:22 — "Do not merely listen to the word, and so deceive yourselves. Do what it says."

SYNOPSIS: Two men at a health club start a conversation. One knows about all the equipment and the best methods of training and comes in every day, but he never actually works out. A statement at the end points out how we need to be more than mere hearers of the Word.

CHARACTERS: Kevin — enthusiastic, very knowledgeable but reluctant to actually exercise
Terry — friendly, doesn't know as much as Kevin about the club and equipment but works out regularly
Narrator

COSTUMES: Sweatsuits or other athletic attire.

PROPS: A couple of towels to hang around Kevin and Terry's necks.

SETTING: A health club. Place an exercise bike Center Stage.

1   *(Scene opens with TERRY riding the exercise bike. He should*
2   *continue riding during the whole sketch. KEVIN comes in.)*
3   **KEVIN:** **Oh wow! You're riding the Rondo 1000 Super**
4   **Pro-line exercise bike. It feels good, doesn't it? It's very**
5   **smooth.**
6   **TERRY:** **It makes my legs hurt.**
7   **KEVIN:** *(Very knowingly)* **Ah yes, but it's a good ache. How**
8   **long have you been on there?**
9   **TERRY:** **Oh, about fifteen minutes.**
10   **KEVIN:** **All you need is twenty minutes of keeping your**
11   **heart rate above one hundred and twenty beats a minute,**
12   **and you are on the road to excellent health. You know,**
13   **you might want to increase the resistance on that bike**
14   **a little to maximize your effort.**
15   **TERRY:** **You sound like you know quite a bit about this stuff.**
16   **KEVIN:** **Well, I try. I love this place; it has all the latest**
17   **equipment: an Olympic-size pool, wide screen videos and**
18   **even a juice bar. The staff here are topnotch. They are**
19   **all in great shape and so knowledgeable. In fact, I'm so**
20   **crazy about this place that I've talked three of my friends**
21   **into joining.**
22   **TERRY:** **That's great. So, what's your favorite piece of**
23   **workout equipment?**
24   **KEVIN:** **I'm partial to the rowing machine myself. It offers**
25   **one of the best total overall workouts. It's good for both**
26   **the cardiovascular system as well as general muscle tone**
27   **and development. It looks like the one machine that I'd**
28   **like to use.**
29   **TERRY:** **What do you mean it "looks" like the one machine**
30   **you'd *like* to use? Which machines do you use?**
31   **KEVIN:** *(Just as cheery)* **I don't really use any of them. There's**
32   **always the danger of overexertion, pulled hamstrings,**
33   **and shin splints. There can be a definite cost to getting**
34   **yourself in shape.**
35   **TERRY:** **But the benefits of being in shape far outweigh the**

1   risk involved.
2 KEVIN: I know. I come here all the time because it's very
3   inspiring to be around people so committed to being in
4   shape.
5 TERRY: But that doesn't help you to get into shape. It's fine
6   to know all about how exercise should be done and to
7   give little tips to others, but that doesn't help you at all.
8   In fact, your advice rings a bit hollow if you haven't
9   actually experienced what you are talking about.
10 KEVIN: Well, it's been nice talking to you. I think I'll mosey
11   on over to the universal gym and . . .
12 TERRY: *(Gets off the bike.)* Hold on a second. How about giving
13   the bike a try before you go? It may be time you actually
14   tried some of this equipment.
15 KEVIN: *(Grimaces.)* I don't know. There's always a danger of
16   falling off.
17 TERRY: Nobody falls off.
18 KEVIN: Actually, one out of every fifty exercise bike users
19   sustains some kind of injury related to falling off.
20 TERRY: How about if I stand beside you and catch you if you
21   tip over?
22 KEVIN: Promise?
23 TERRY: Promise. *(Freeze)*
24 NARRATOR: In Scripture, we are encouraged to not be
25   merely hearers of the word, but doers also. Ministry is
26   the practical application of our faith. And as James wrote
27   so bluntly in his letter in the New Testament, "Faith by
28   itself, if it is not accompanied by action, is dead." [1]
29
30
31
32
33
34
35   [1] *James 2:17*

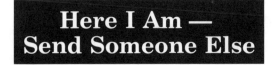

Here I Am —
Send Someone Else

THEME: **Evangelism** — Often we pray for God to send someone to help an acquaintance in need. We may, however, be the answer to our own prayers.

SCRIPTURE: **Isaiah 6:8** — "Then I heard the voice of the Lord saying, 'Whom shall I send? And who will go for us?' And I said, 'Here am I. Send me!' "
Matthew 28:19 — "Go and make disciples of all nations, baptizing them in the name of the Father and of the Son and of the Holy Spirit."

SYNOPSIS: While praying that God will send someone to work in the life of a neighbor, Bill hears from God that he may be the answer to his own prayer.

CHARACTERS: Bill/Betsy — a person who is pious in words but not in deeds
Voice of God (Off-stage)

COSTUMES: Bathrobe or P.J.s

PROPS: None.

SETTING: Bill's (or Betsy's) bedroom. The bed may be pantomimed, or you may put a pillow and blanket on a pew or the piano bench.

"Listen, God, if you don't mind, I'd like to get back to my prayer."

1   *(Scene opens with BILL kneeling in prayer at the side of his bed.)*

2   **BILL:** Dear heavenly Father, I bring before you this evening

3   my dear neighbor Ramsey Wilson. Thou knowest how he

4   needeth you-eth in his life-eth. Grant that he may find a

5   friend who could point him to you . . .

6   **GOD:** *(From Off-stage)* What about you?

7   **BILL:** What about me?

8   **GOD:** Why don't *you* point Ramsey Wilson to me?

9   **BILL:** What do you mean?

10   **GOD:** Well, you are the one with the concern for Ramsey. It

11   seems to me that you'd be perfect for the job.

12   **BILL:** But — but — we don't have anything in common.

13   **GOD:** You both watch *Wheel of Fortune.*

14   **BILL:** Really?

15   **GOD:** Really.

16   **BILL:** OK, but how am I going to get the conversation from

17   Vanna to you? I don't think it would work.

18   **GOD:** Well, you're both on the same bowling team. That's

19   something you have in common.

20   **BILL:** But God, who has time to talk in the middle of bowling?

1   GOD: You could go out for coffee afterwards. Bill, just spend
2   some time with Ramsey. I'm doing all the behind-the-
3   scenes work like preparing his heart and convincing him
4   of his need. It's all set up for you.
5   BILL: I don't have the time.
6   GOD: Pardon me?
7   BILL: You heard me. I said, "I don't have the time." Look, it's
8   easy for you to say "Spend time with Ramsey." You've
9   got all the time in the world! I have to prioritize my time.
10   GOD: I guess I thought that because of your prayer, Ramsey
11   *was* a priority.
12   BILL: Well, it's always easy to find time to pray for someone,
13   but it takes a real commitment to actually get out and
14   do something.
15   GOD: I couldn't have said it any better myself.
16   BILL: Oh no! Look at the time. Listen God, if you don't mind,
17   I'd like to get back to my prayer. I'm behind schedule
18   and I'd like to ask you for a few more things before I go
19   to bed.
20   GOD: Well, think it over, Bill. And remember that I am the
21   one who gave you the concern for Ramsey in the first
22   place.
23   BILL: Here I am, God. Send someone else . . .
24
25
26
27
28
29
30
31
32
33
34
35

Job Review at the Pizza De-Lite

THEME: **Judgment** — As believers, we will stand before the judgment throne of God. But if we have been living a life guided by the Word of God, it is not something that we need to fear.

SCRIPTURE: **Matthew 25:34, 41** — "Then the King will say to those on his right, 'Come, you who are blessed by my father, take your inheritance, the kingdom prepared for you since the creation of the world.' Then he will say to those on his left, 'Depart from me, you who are cursed, into the eternal fire . . .' "

SYNOPSIS: The manager of the Pizza De-Lite finds that one of her best employees, Mindy, is worried about her job review that afternoon. The manager points out that Mindy has nothing to worry about as she has been a responsible and reliable worker. Likewise, we have nothing to fear about judgment if we believe in Jesus and have been living our lives by his Word.

CHARACTERS: Penny — Cheerful, encouraging manager, rather motherly
Mindy — Teenager, concerned about her job

COSTUMES: Fast-food-type uniforms, if desired, or just hats and name tags.

PROPS: Dish towels, large cardboard box.

SETTING: Pizza restaurant. No set pieces needed.

"I have a job review with the boss today?"

1	*(Scene opens with MINDY rummaging around in a box trying*
2	*to find dish towels. She is sighing and obviously upset about*
3	*something. PENNY enters drying her hands on a dish towel.)*
4	**PENNY: Mindy, what's the matter?**
5	**MINDY:** *(Sigh)* **Oh, Penny, you won't believe what just**
6	**happened a few minutes ago. I . . .**
7	**PENNY:** *(Interrupting)* **You can tell me. I'm your manager here**
8	**at Pizza De-Lite and I care about you and your problems.**
9	**MINDY: Well, I'm worried because I just . . .**
10	**PENNY:** *(Interrupting)* **Oh, Mindy, are you concerned about**
11	**your job review with the boss this afternoon?**
12	**MINDY:** *(Shocked)* **I have a job review with the boss today?**
13	**Oh, no!**
14	**PENNY: Now, don't worry, Mindy. Everyone who works here**
15	**has a job review with the boss every six months. It's no**
16	**big deal.**
17	**MINDY: But you don't understand! Just now I . . .**
18	**PENNY: Mindy, Mindy, Mindy, I do understand. That's why**
19	**I am a manager.**
20	**MINDY: But Penny, just now . . .** *(In the following lines, MINDY*

1		*and PENNY should interrupt each other. Their lines should flow*
2		*one right after the other in rapid succession.)*
3	PENNY:	Listen to me, Mindy . . .
4	MINDY:	. . . out on the floor . . .
5	PENNY:	. . . you are one of our best workers . . .
6	MINDY:	. . . I carried two pitchers of coke . . .
7	PENNY:	. . . you are very responsible . . .
8	MINDY:	. . . and a large anchovy Pizza De-Lite pizza
9		special . . .
10	PENNY:	. . . you're reliable . . .
11	MINDY:	. . . to the *boss and his family* . . .
12	PENNY:	. . . so you have nothing to be afraid of . . .
13	MINDY:	. . . and I tripped and dumped it all on his lap . . .
14	PENNY:	You have lots to be afraid of. You dumped two
15		pitchers of pop and a large pizza in the boss's lap?
16	MINDY:	Yes, it was a terrible accident. Now I'm afraid that
17		he'll fire me.
18	PENNY:	Mindy, it was an accident. He'll understand.
19	MINDY:	Do you think so?
20	PENNY:	I do.
21	MINDY:	But what about my job review? The boss is the last
22		person I want to sit down and talk to today!
23	PENNY:	You have nothing to be worried about. You are a
24		conscientious and responsible worker. You are
25		committed to the company, and you try to do your job
26		right. After reviewing your work, the boss will probably
27		tell you how great you are and give you a raise.
28	MINDY:	That makes me feel much better. Well, I'd better get
29		back out there.
30	PENNY:	See? What a great attitude. Are you going to wait on
31		some more tables?
32	MINDY:	Not yet. The boss sent me back here to get these
33		towels so that he can wipe himself off. *(Freeze)*
34		
35		

Let's Make a Tithe Deal

THEME: **Giving** — So often our ability to give financially is determined more by our attitude than by our financial position.

SCRIPTURE: **Malachi 3:8** — "Will a man rob God? Yet you rob me. But you ask, 'how do we rob you?' 'In tithes and offerings.' "
Mark 12:41-44, Luke 21:1-4 — Story of the widow and her two mites.

SYNOPSIS: Two couples on a game show are both eager to give a tithe of their income to the Lord. However, one couple keeps waiting for the right time. By the end of the game, they still haven't given a cent.

CHARACTERS: Bob Darker — game show host
Alice and Frank Ford
Oscar and Mary Meyers

COSTUMES: Suit and tie for Bob.

PROPS: Six large cards (8½" x 5½") with "Life Situations" written on them.

SETTING: The set of a television game show. Place a podium Center Stage for Bob (or he may use the pulpit).

"A fixed income? What about all my investments?"

1 (*Scene opens with couples in place on either side of the host.*
2 *BOB's responses should all be equally enthusiastic regardless of*
3 *the tithe response.*)
4 BOB: Good evening. I'm Bob Darker, and welcome to "Let's
5   Make a Tithe Deal," the game show that imitates real life
6   to find out how we tithe. Couple number one, tell us who
7   you are.
8 FRANK: Hi, Bob. I'm Frank Ford, and this is my wife Alice.
9 BOB: And couple number two?
10 MARY: Hi, Bob. I'm Mary Meyers, and this is my husband
11   Oscar.
12 BOB: I'm glad to know you, folks. Well, let's get started. I will
13   read real life situations to you. It will be the same for
14   both couples. You tell me *your* tithe response. Here we
15   go with card number one. It says, "You're in the twenty
16   to thirty age bracket, no kids, just getting started." What
17   is your tithe response, Frank?
18 FRANK: Well, if we're just getting started, I'd say we'll need
19   to buy those basic things like a stereo, a car, and
20   hopefully, a house.

1   ALICE: Don't forget paying off our college education.

2   FRANK: Right. Um . . . we'll pass for now, but in the future

3   we'll tithe.

4   BOB: Fine. How about you, Oscar?

5   OSCAR: I agree with what Frank said, but I think we want to

6   get started right. So . . . we'll tithe.

7   BOB: OK! Well, card number two reads, "You're thirty to

8   forty-five years old and you bought a house in the

9   suburbs. You have a cat, a dog, and 2.4 kids." Oscar and

10   Mary, what is your tithe response?

11   MARY: It sounds like it's gonna take a lot of money to live

12   under those circumstances, but our church is important

13   and it helps our family. I guess our giving is one way to

14   teach the kids what's important too. Yeah, we'll tithe.

15   BOB: Great. Frank and Alice, what is your tithe response?

16   ALICE: Well, you know having a house means constant

17   repairs. And a growing family is expensive with shoes

18   and clothes, dentist bills, dancing and music lessons,

19   baseball, soccer, lacrosse, hockey, football and croquet

20   uniforms and pads. Doggonit Bob, I think we'll have to

21   wait and tithe in the future.

22   BOB: Fine. Card number three: "Your kids are in college and

23   your income is at an all-time high." Frank and Alice, what

24   is your tithe response?

25   FRANK: Well, on the surface it sounds good, Bob. But we

26   made too much money last year. The government won't

27   offer us any aid to send the kids to college.

28   ALICE: Right. We're footing the entire bill!

29   FRANK: Plus, we're in a higher tax bracket, and we need to

30   think about paying off the house and the summer cottage.

31   ALICE: We may even have to cut back.

32   FRANK: I think we'll wait and tithe in the future.

33   ALICE: We're definitely getting closer to tithing, though!

34   FRANK: Definitely!

35   BOB: How about you two, Oscar and Mary?

1   OSCAR: I think that's an easy one, Bob. Expenses are up, but
2   so is income. We're making more than we ever have. We'll
3   tithe!
4   BOB: OK, card number four says, "You're fifty-five to sixty-
5   five and your income is at a respectable level." Oscar and
6   Mary, what is your tithe response?
7   MARY: Well, we want to continue to be faithful. Besides, we
8   have grandkids benefitting from the church's ministry
9   now.
10   OSCAR: And we want to continue helping others. God has
11   been good. We'll keep on tithing.
12   BOB: Super! Frank and Alice?
13   ALICE: Well, Bob, I really thought it was gonna happen this
14   time, but we're looking at retirement soon.
15   FRANK: We've got to put money away for that.
16   ALICE: And we have to help the kids get started with their
17   first homes and things like that.
18   FRANK: I think we'll have to pass for now, but it's safe to
19   say that in the very near future, it will work to tithe.
20   BOB: Okey-dokey! Card number five reads, "You're sixty-five
21   and older on a fixed income." Frank and Alice, what is
22   your tithe response?
23   FRANK: *(Horrified)* A fixed income? What about all my
24   investments?
25   ALICE: It's only a game, dear. Bob, with inflation and all that,
26   we're gonna need every penny. We'll pass just this one
27   time. But we will definitely tithe in the future.
28   FRANK: Yes, you can write that down.
29   ALICE: Count on it!
30   BOB: OK. Oscar and Mary, what is your tithe response?
31   MARY: Well, the fixed income means our total giving will go
32   down, but I think we'll still want to give a percentage.
33   What do you think, honey?
34   OSCAR: Oh, yeah, I think we can still give. I don't want to
35   stop doing something important *now* that we've been

1   doing all our lives. We'll tithe.

2 BOB: Well, that's the game folks! Oscar and Mary, you have

3   given thousands and thousands of dollars over the years.

4   And Frank and Alice . . .

5 FRANK: *(Interrupting)* Wait, this isn't fair! I didn't have a

6   chance to give.

7 ALICE: Yeah, what about a balloon tithe? You know — one

8   *mega* tithe.

9 FRANK: Hey, you've got one more card. What does it say?

10 ALICE: Yeah, give us a chance. We didn't know the game was

11   gonna end!

12 BOB: Well, the card says, "You died."

13 FRANK: *(Triumphantly)* That's OK, I'll leave my estate to the

14   church!

15 ALICE: That's what we've been planning all along.

16 FRANK: That's right, all along.

17 BOB: You didn't let me finish. It says, "You died and your

18   estate was sold to pay for bad investments in downhill

19   ski resorts in Iowa."

20 FRANK: I invested in that? I did *that?* *(ALICE and FRANK*

21   *ad-lib arguing.)*

22 BOB: And that's the show. Oscar and Mary have lived a

23   responsible faithful life of good stewardship. Frank and

24   Alice . . . well, you know how that goes. Until next week —

25   happy tithing!

26

27

28

29

30

31

32

33

34

35

Live! With Brock Tully

THEME: The Sermon on the Mount

SCRIPTURE: Matthew 5-7

SYNOPSIS: A woman is interviewed by a slightly confused TV personality. In the course of the interview, a basic introduction to the Sermon on the Mount is given.

CHARACTERS: Rachel — well-meaning but dry woman who listened attentively to Jesus when he spoke
Brock Tully — TV interviewer, rather brash and confident (aren't they all?)
Gil — announcer (Off-stage voice)

COSTUMES: Contemporary clothes. Trenchcoat for Brock.

PROPS: Microphone, some kind of handiwork for Rachel to do.

SETTING: A street in Jerusalem. Set a chair Upstage Left for Rachel.

1   *(Scene opens with BROCK TULLY Down Center Stage facing*
2   *forward. RACHEL is Upstage to his left, crocheting, knitting,*
3   *or etc.).*
4   GIL: *(From Off-stage)* ... And that's it for the local news. We
5   now take you to our man on the street reporter, Brock
6   Tully, who is uncovering all the news in the Holy City.
7   Over to you, Brock.
8   BROCK: Thanks, Gil. Yes, I'm Brock Tully, reporting to you
9   live from Jerusalem, the Holy City. Jesus of Nazareth
10   has just recently been through here on a speaking tour,
11   and I have been interviewing some of the locals to find
12   out their responses to this curious man. *(Steps back beside*
13   *RACHEL.)* With me today is Sarah Bahtjacob ...
14   RACHEL: That's Rachel ...
15   BROCK: Rachel Bahtjacob. Rachel, it's 28 A.D., you are on a
16   hot, dusty road outside of Jericho, and Jesus heals a man
17   born blind. What's going through your mind?
18   RACHEL: Nothing. I wasn't there when Jesus healed the
19   blind man.. I was at the series of talks he gave up north
20   in Capernaum.
21   BROCK: Ah yes, the talks he gave on the Mount of Olives.
22   RACHEL: No, the Mount of Olives is right here — just
23   outside of Jerusalem. When I heard Jesus, he was up on
24   one of the hills of black basalt that rise almost right out
25   of the Sea of Galilee.
26   BROCK: Right. So, Rebecca ...
27   RACHEL: Rachel ...
28   BROCK: Rachel, it's 28 A.D., you are on a hot, dusty hillside
29   outside of Capernaum, and Jesus preaches for hours.
30   What's going through your mind?
31   RACHEL: I can't see him.
32   BROCK: You can't see him?
33   RACHEL: He's a rabbi — a teacher — so he sits down when
34   he teaches. There were so many people standing in front
35   of me — most of the town had come to hear him speak —

1   that I really didn't get a good look at him. I could hear

2   him, though.

3 BROCK: So, Rawanda, what did he say?

4 RACHEL: It's Rachel. Jesus said that he hadn't come to get

5   rid of the law or the prophets, but to fulfill them. Then

6   he gave principles, ideals and motives for conduct.

7 BROCK: What did the people think of that?

8 RACHEL: At first his principles for living sounded too hard

9   to measure up to — especially compared to the law we

10   were brought up with. But the more he taught us, the

11   more we were able to see that following his higher

12   standards could lead to a better lifestyle.

13 BROCK: Can you tell us anything about the themes Jesus

14   spoke on, Reumah?

15 RACHEL: It's Rachel. Jesus talked quite a bit about the

16   kingdom of heaven, the high call of being one of his

17   disciples, living the right life before God and man, and

18   the dangers of getting sidetracked.

19 BROCK: I see. Well, we're almost out of time. Thanks Rahab,

20   for your eyewitness account. *(Looking in the direction GIL's*

21   *Off-stage voice comes from)* There you have it, Gil. In a series

22   of talks on the big, black basalt hills of Capernaum, Jesus

23   raised the standards for being a follower of God. I'm

24   Brock Tully in the Holy City. Back to you, Gil.

25

26

27

28

29

30

31

32

33

34

35

Lost in the Great White North

THEME: **Evangelism** — Our reluctance to share our faith can be disastrous.

SCRIPTURE: **Matthew 4:16** — "Let your light shine before men, that they may see your good deeds and praise your father in heaven."

SYNOPSIS: The party of a downed plane is "lost" one at a time in the dark because the one person with a flashlight doesn't want to share it with the others.

CHARACTERS: Captain — all business
Stewardess — on the ditsy side
Willis — crew member
Zwick — crew member
Johnson — crew member without a clue
Narrator

COSTUMES: The Captain may wear a captain's cap and blue blazer. The Stewardess should be dressed up (e.g., coordinated suit).

PROPS: Matches, flashlight. You can add a lot to this sketch by using kids for props (bear, trees, rock).

SETTING: The Great White North. If possible, dim the lights so the flashlight shows up better.

"We lost Willis, sir. I think a bear got him."

1 (*Scene opens with the group lined up single file at the back of*
2 *the sanctuary in the following order: CAPTAIN, STEWARD-*
3 *ESS, ZWICK, WILLIS, and JOHNSON at the rear. They blindly*
4 *follow the CAPTAIN up the aisle, slowly working their way to*
5 *the front throughout the sketch. If kids are playing the bear, tree,*
6 *and rock, they should be seated in pews that are close to the aisle*
7 *and several rows apart. They then spring up at the appropriate*
8 *time.*)
9 **WILLIS:** **Boy, it's so dark. Do you know where you're going,**
10 **Captain?**
11 **CAPTAIN:** **OK, folks, I admit it. We're lost.**
12 **ALL:** (*Ad-libbing despairing moans and groans.*) **Oh no. Say it**
13 **isn't true!** (*Etc.*)
14 **STEWARDESS:** **I sure wish our plane hadn't crashed!**
15 **CAPTAIN:** **Well, we had no choice but to crash land after our**
16 **engines fell off. But we have one last chance.**
17 **ZWICK:** **What's that, sir?**
18 **CAPTAIN:** **Just before the sun went down, I saw a creek**
19 **below us. If we can get to that creek, I know we can follow**
20 **it to civilization. But getting down there is going to be**

1   **dangerous. Does anyone have any kind of light?**
2   *(JOHNSON, at the back of the line, flashes his flashlight around*
3   *but says nothing.)*
4   **STEWARDESS:** *(Loudly)* **I have some matches!**
5   **CAPTAIN: Matches?! Great! What luck!** *(ZWICK and WILLIS*
6   *congratulate her.)*
7   **WILLIS: Fantastic! Now we have a sporting chance.**
8   **ZWICK: Let's go for it, Captain!**
9   **CAPTAIN: OK, we're off.** *(As the CAPTAIN strikes a match, they*
10   *all hurry forward and then stop as it dies. JOHNSON then pulls*
11   *out a flashlight and points it at the ground.)*
12   **STEWARDESS: It's so hard to see.** *(An imaginary or kid bear*
13   *growls and pulls WILLIS off to the side.)*
14   **WILLIS: Aaahhh!**
15   **CAPTAIN: What was that?**
16   **ZWICK: We lost Willis, sir. I think a bear got him.**
17   **CAPTAIN: Well, let's press on. Everyone else OK? Johnson?**
18   **JOHNSON:** *(Smugly)* **Fine, sir. Couldn't be better!** *(They move*
19   *forward. The CAPTAIN ducks, and then the STEWARDESS*
20   *ducks, but ZWICK doesn't, and he hits his head on an imaginary*
21   *tree branch or on someone posed as a tree.)*
22   **ZWICK: Aaahhh ...** *(Falls to the side.)*
23   **CAPTAIN: Oh no, not another one!**
24   **STEWARDESS: Captain, I think Zwick didn't see the branch.**
25   **CAPTAIN:** *(Despair)* **Oh, no. We lost Zwick. He was the best**
26   **bathroom attendant we ever had work for our airline.**
27   **Well, let's stick together. Johnson, you amaze me. You**
28   **must have great night vision to be at the back, yet see**
29   **better than Zwick or Willis!**
30   **JOHNSON: Well, sometime I'll tell you about it, sir.**
31   **CAPTAIN: Let's stick close together. We're almost out of**
32   **matches.** *(They walk forward. STEWARDESS immediately*
33   *trips and falls over the "rock," rolling away as if down the*
34   *mountain. She makes no noise. JOHNSON stops and shines his*
35   *light down on her and then walks by. The CAPTAIN mutters to*

1   *to himself.)* **We should almost be there. I can hear the creek.**
2   **Rats, that was the last match . . . We're in trouble,**
3   **Johnson! I can't see a thing. I . . . Oooh, no!** *(Falls and rolls*
4   *to the side. JOHNSON walks past with the flashlight.)* **Johnson,**
5   **Johnson, help me . . .**
6   JOHNSON: **Where are you, sir?**
7   CAPTAIN: **Over here.**
8   JOHNSON: *(Turns around and shines the flashlight on him.)* **Oh,**
9   **there you are.**
10 CAPTAIN: **You have a flashlight?**
11 JOHNSON: **Sure do, and it's a dandy!**
12 CAPTAIN: **Why in thunderation didn't you tell us when we**
13   **asked if anyone had a light?**
14 JOHNSON: **Well, you didn't ask specifically for a flashlight.**
15   **I didn't want to impose, and you all seemed so excited**
16   **about the matches.**
17 CAPTAIN: **But you had a *better* light!**
18 JOHNSON: **I was kind of hoping that maybe you'd just notice**
19   **my light and ask me about it.**
20 CAPTAIN: **Well, Johnson, I know we would've asked if we**
21   **could've seen it!** *(Freeze)*
22 NARRATOR: **"You are the light of the world. A city on a hill**
23   **cannot be hidden. Neither do people light a lamp and put**
24   **it under a bowl. Instead they put it on its stand, and it**
25   **gives light to everyone in the house. In the same way, let**
26   **your light shine before men, that they may see your good**
27   **deeds and praise your Father in heaven."** [1]
28
29
30
31
32
33
34
35   [1] *Matthew 5:14-16*

Mary's Story

THEME: **Christmas** — Jesus was born of a woman who was young but devout in her relationship to God. Mary was an actual, historic figure.

SCRIPTURE: **Luke 1:26-38, 2:1-7** — The account of Jesus' birth.

SYNOPSIS: Mary recounts the story of the angel's visit and the subsequent events leading to Jesus' birth.

CHARACTERS: Mary, the mother of Jesus — Should be portrayed by a girl 13 to 17 years of age, demure but articulate.

COSTUMES: Long biblical robe and a scarf about 12 inches wide and 36 inches long, draped loosely around her face, sandals.

PROPS: None.

SETTING: Biblical times.

(MARY *relates the story shyly at first but gaining confidence as she becomes caught up in remembering the details. A nice touch, if the actress is confident, is to have her hold a one-year-old child. Telling the story while trying to keep a squirming baby occupied gives a wonderful background to the script.*)

MARY: I was fourteen when the parents of the village carpenter, Joseph, approached my parents about marriage. "Joseph needs a wife," they said, "and Mary is a serious girl who loves the law and God. We would like her to marry Joseph." So the arrangements were made and I became engaged to Joseph, the quiet, steady, devout village carpenter. He was twenty-nine years old.

I was excited to be getting married. Most of my friends were already having children. Usually about a year would pass before the marriage actually took place, so Joseph and I began to spend some time getting to know each other.

We had been engaged about three months when the most troubling event occurred. I was all alone preparing the evening meal for my father and brothers when an angel appeared! He said I had found favor with God and that I was to give birth to the *Messiah!*

Ever since I was a child, I had prayed for the coming of the Promised One, the Messiah, to lead Israel. But, how could it be that I, who had no husband yet, could have a child? He told me the Holy Spirit would cause a baby to grow within me. I felt fear, terror and joy all at once. But I told the angel, "I am the Lord's servant, may it be to me as you have said." Then the angel left.

One morning, about a week later, I woke up sick to my stomach! I, the one who was to be the mother of the Messiah, had morning sickness something awful! I guess I should have expected it because I remember my sisters had all had it when they were expecting. It was then that I realized I really was going to have a baby.

1   The angel had said that my cousin Elizabeth was
2 going to have a baby too, so I went to stay with her for
3 awhile. Elizabeth believed my story, much to my relief,
4 for I had told no one. The time that I spent with her was
5 wonderful. She understood better than anyone else what
6 I was going through. She also fed me lots of bagels to
7 settle my upset stomach from the morning sickness.
8   After three months, I went home. The next few
9 weeks were terrible. My family could tell right away that
10 I was pregnant. They wanted to believe my story, but it
11 was too fantastic. They talked with Joseph, and he
12 decided to quietly break off the engagement. I was
13 crushed. Who would want me now with a child? But you
14 know, I trusted that God would make things work out —
15 after all, it was his Son that was growing inside me.
16 *(Growing excitement)* And God did work it out! One
17 afternoon Joseph came to my parents and me and said
18 that an angel had appeared to him in a dream! The angel
19 told Joseph that the child was God's and that Joseph
20 should not be afraid to marry me. I was so happy!
21   As the baby grew, everyone in the village became
22 aware that I was pregnant. There was some very vicious
23 gossip about Joseph and me, but it didn't bother me now.
24 My parents and Joseph knew the truth and supported me.
25   When Caesar issued the decree that an official
26 census was to be taken, I didn't think much about it. But
27 as the week approached when Joseph and I were to leave
28 for Bethlehem, I realized my due date would be the day
29 of our arrival there. It is ninety miles to Bethlehem —
30 three long days on a donkey. I was so tired and
31 uncomfortable. We slept outside at night, and I just
32 couldn't get comfortable there, either.
33   On the third day as we neared Bethlehem, there, on
34 the back of a donkey, I had my first labor pains. Joseph
35 used his sundial to see how far apart they were. By the

time we reached the city, it was dark. Because of the census, there were people everywhere and all the inns were full. The contractions were so close together, the pain would shoot through my whole body. I almost fell off the donkey. I was glad it was dark. No one could see the tears running down my cheeks nor hear the little cries of pain that escaped from my clenched teeth. Poor Joseph was going crazy. This normally quiet, sedate man was running in and out of inns trying to find me a bed. It seemed so absurd. Was the Messiah, the Son of God, to be born on a street with not even a wall to shelter him from the night wind?

At last Joseph found something — a stable, a little barn on the back of an inn. Joseph kept saying, "It won't be too bad. It won't be too bad." But when we stepped inside, there was no kidding around. It was bad. It *was* a barn. But I was just grateful to finally have a place to lie down. The dirt, the smell, the animals, the bugs, it didn't matter — I had a baby *demanding* to be born; and if this was where God wanted his son to come into the world, then this was where it would happen.

Shortly after midnight, Jesus was born. I don't remember much except a lot of pain and then a baby crying. Joseph said that every time I would moan from the pain, the cows would moo and the sheep would baa! I was exhausted. Later in the night, some shepherds came to see Jesus. They knew that even though he was just a baby, there was something very special about my child.

My first son, Jesus. Once I held him in my arms, I realized that I would go through the pain, shame and fear of those past nine months all over again if God wanted it. I had a son. But more importantly, the world now had a Savior.

I was just a fifteen-year-old mother. Just another Jewish girl who tried to live a life pleasing to God, yet he chose me to have his son, Jesus, the Messiah.

A Matter of Height

THEME: **Spiritual maturity** — We do not just naturally mature as Christians. Time is important, but it is also necessary to know the Word of God and to practice it.

SCRIPTURE: **Hebrews 6:1** — "Let us leave the elementary teachings about Christ and go on to maturity . . ."

SYNOPSIS: In a world where height is a measure of Christian maturity, a man goes into a hardware store that is staffed by a quite tall individual. The basic steps to growth as a Christian are covered in their conversation.

CHARACTERS: Nolan — Hardware store clerk, quite tall
Bill — Customer, should be shorter than Nolan (the greater the difference in height, the better the visual humor)
Narrator

COSTUMES: A plain, bib-style apron for Nolan.

PROPS: Miscellaneous hardware and a piece of paper for the list.

SETTING: A hardware store. Set a rectangular table Center Stage to serve as a counter. (Place it vertically so the congregation views the actors from the side.)

1   *(Scene opens with NOLAN puttering around in the store. BILL*
2   *comes in to buy a screwdriver.)*
3   **NARRATOR:**   The issue of maturity as a Christian can be so
4   confusing. Wouldn't it be nice if the more Christ-like you
5   were, the taller you grew? What if *height* was the
6   indicator of spiritual maturity?
7   **BILL:**   *(Looking at a list and talking as he enters)* **Hey, do you sell**
8   stepladders? I'm having trouble reaching some stuff. And
9   I need one of those electric screwdrivers. Also, I . . . wow,
10   you must be a Christian!
11   **NOLAN:**   *(Amazed)* **That's right. How could you tell?**
12   **BILL:**   *(Looking him up and down)* **Because you're so tall.**
13   Everybody knows that the more mature you are as a
14   Christian, the taller you grow. *(Shakes his head.)* **You must**
15   be almost as tall as Billy Graham!
16   **NOLAN:**   Well, not quite. What can I help you find?
17   **BILL:**   The first thing I need is an electric screwdriver. Do
18   you carry those?
19   **NOLAN:**   Yes, and I think we even have a few on sale. Let me
20   look around here a bit.
21   **BILL:**   *(Conversationally)* **How long have you been a Christian?**
22   **NOLAN:**   *(While looking behind the counter)* **Oh, about six years.**
23   **BILL:**   Six years!
24   **NOLAN:**   *(Looks over the counter.)* **What's the matter?**
25   **BILL:**   *I've* **been a Christian six years.**
26   **NOLAN:**   Oh . . . *(Looks behind the counter again.)* **Ah, here we go**
27   . . . oh, no, that's not it . . .
28   **BILL:**   So you must be pretty tall for your spiritual age.
29   **NOLAN:**   Not really. You should see my brother. He's been a
30   Christian for only two years, but he started doing some
31   serious study of the Bible, and *(Looks over counter at BILL)*
32   he's grown five inches in the last three months.
33   **BILL:**   Five inches!
34   **NOLAN:**   The Boston Celtics have been trying to get him to
35   play basketball for them.

1   **BILL:**   *(Sits on the stool.)* **Five inches in three months. I must be**
2   **doing something wrong. How can you and I be the same**
3   **age as Christians but so different in height?**
4   **NOLAN:**   *(Stands up.)* **Maybe you're not growing *up* as a**
5   **Christian — maybe you're just growing *old*.**
6   **BILL:**   **Well, there is no doubt that I am growing old. But**
7   **don't we just naturally mature as we age?**
8   **NOLAN:**   **Hopefully as you get older you mature, but there are**
9   **two other important considerations as well.**
10   **BILL:**   **Can those two things help me grow tall enough to**
11   **change the lightbulbs in my ceiling without using a**
12   **chair?**
13   **NOLAN:**   **They can.**
14   **BILL:**   *(Rubs his hands together in anticipation.)* **Then fire away,**
15   **I'm listening.**
16   **NOLAN:**   **Well, like you said, we mature over time, but we also**
17   **must become accustomed to the Word of God.**
18   **BILL:**   **Which is found in the Bible.**
19   **NOLAN:**   **Right. But that isn't enough. We must practice the**
20   **Word of God. We need to put into action the things we**
21   **learn.**
22   **BILL:**   *(Dubiously)* **And that's how you got so tall?**
23   **NOLAN:**   **It sure is. Six years ago I was just a little less tall**
24   **than you. How many inches have you grown in the last**
25   **six years?**
26   **BILL:**   **Yeah, well, I . . .** *(Looks at his watch.)* **Hey, I've got to run!**
27   **Do you have the screwdriver or not?**
28   **NOLAN:**   **I'm afraid we're all out. Do you still need a stepladder?**
29   **BILL:**   **No. After the things you've told me, I don't think I'll**
30   **be needing it. But I may still need a footstool for awhile.**
31   **Do you have one of those?** *(Freeze)*
32
33
34
35

The Music Teacher

THEME: **Attitude** — We reap what we sow in life.

SCRIPTURE: **Matthew 13:1-9, Luke 8:4-8, 11-15** — The parable of the sower and the seed.

SYNOPSIS: A woman who has been a piano teacher for many years tells a prospective student about the different types of students she has had. The four kinds of students correspond to the four types of soil and four different responses to hearing the word of God.

CHARACTERS: Jo Ann Wilson — The piano teacher, confident and firm
Debbie — Excited, enthusiastic about taking lessons, a little "dizzy"
Narrator

COSTUMES: Conservative outfit for Jo Ann, trendy outfit for Debbie.

PROPS: Stacks of music books and a group picture in a 8" by 10" picture frame.

SETTING: A piano lesson. If possible, stage this sketch by your church's piano. Set the framed picture and music books on top of it.

"Wow! I am, like, so incredibly excited to meet you."

1   **NARRATOR:**   **While a large crowd was gathering and people**
2   **were coming to Jesus from town after town, he told this**
3   **parable: "A farmer went out to sow his seed. As he was**
4   **scattering the seed, some fell along the path; it was**
5   **trampled on, and the birds of the air ate it up. Some fell**
6   **on rock, and when it came up, the plants withered because**
7   **they had no moisture. Other seed fell among thorns, which**
8   **grew up with it and choked the plants. Still other seed fell**
9   **on good soil. It came up and yielded a crop, a hundred**
10   **times more than was sown." When he saw this, he called**
11   **out, "He who has ears to hear, let him hear."** [1]
12   *(Scene opens with JO ANN standing by the piano, humming to*
13   *herself and looking through some music books. DEBBIE knocks*
14   *on the door.)*
15   **JO ANN:**   **Come in.**
16   **DEBBIE:**   **Wow! Are you Jo Ann Wilson?**
17   **JO ANN:**   **Yes, I am.**
18   **DEBBIE:**   **Wow! I am, like, so incredibly excited to meet you.**
19   **My name is Debbie.**
20   [1] *Luke 8:4-8*

1   **JO ANN:**   **I am pleased to meet you Debbie. How can I ...**

2   **DEBBIE:**   *(Somewhat awestruck as she interrupts JO ANN)* **Is this**

3   **the room where you write your music?**

4   **JO ANN:**   **Well, sometimes. Mostly I teach piano students in**

5   **this room. Is that what you're here for — piano lessons?**

6   **DEBBIE:**   **That's right. I want to play piano as well as you do.**

7   **JO ANN:**   **So you've heard me play?**

8   **DEBBIE:**   **I sure have. I heard you do a concert at the Lincoln**

9   **Center** *(Or substitute local performance hall)* **last Thursday**

10   **night and the music made me feel so good that I decided**

11   **that I would play the piano too.**

12   **JO ANN:**   **Have you ever ...**

13   **DEBBIE:**   *(Spots picture.)* **Oh, wow! Are these all the students**

14   **you've had?**

15   **JO ANN:**   **Actually I've had many more students, but that is**

16   **one group I started with a couple of years ago.**

17   **DEBBIE:**   *(Dreamy)* **And now all those people play piano just**

18   **like you ...**

19   **JO ANN:**   **No, not really.**

20   **DEBBIE:**   **But you taught them, didn't you?**

21   **JO ANN:**   **I tried, but there is more to it than just having a**

22   **good teacher. Just like you, all those people came here**

23   **for lessons because they had heard me play. They decided**

24   **that they wanted to play piano too.**

25   **DEBBIE:**   **So what happened to them?**

26   **JO ANN:**   **Well, this fellow here** *(Points to the picture)* **wanted to**

27   **play, but he decided that he didn't need a teacher. He**

28   **thought he could teach himself to play. He was a pretty**

29   **proud young man.**

30   **DEBBIE:**   **Wow. That's sad. I'm glad I know I need a teacher.**

31   **JO ANN:**   **This girl showed great promise and enthusiasm,**

32   **but after a couple of months she dropped out when**

33   **practicing became too much work for her.**

34   **DEBBIE:**   *(Hedging a bit)* **Well, no one really** *likes* **to practice ...**

35   **JO ANN:**   **But the discipline is necessary if you want to play.**

1 DEBIE: *(Changing the subject)* **What about this guy? He's cute?**

2 JO ANN: **That young man practiced regularly and gave the**

3 **piano his full attention for almost a year. He was doing**

4 **great. I thought he would become a fine player, but**

5 **gradually other things took priority.**

6 DEBBIE: **Oh, I know him! He plays guitar for a rap band now.**

7 JO ANN: *(Dryly)* **I'm sad to hear that he has left music**

8 **altogether.**

9 DEBBIE: **So** *none* **of these people play piano now?**

10 JO ANN: **No, many of them do. Some of them have become**

11 **very accomplished players. They kept their priorities.**

12 **From the time when they first heard my music and**

13 **decided to learn to play, they have kept at it. They have**

14 **matured as musicians.**

15 DEBBIE: *(Wide-eyed innocence)* **Wow! I'd like to be mature.**

16 JO ANN: **Well, then, let's talk about you and piano lessons.**

17 *(Freeze)*

18 NARRATOR: **This is the meaning of the parable: The seed**

19 **is the Word of God. Those along the path are the ones**

20 **who hear, and then the devil comes and takes away the**

21 **Word from their hearts, so that they may not believe and**

22 **be saved. Those on the rock are the ones who receive the**

23 **Word with joy when they hear it, but they have no root.**

24 **They believe for awhile, but in the time of testing they**

25 **fall away. The seed that fell among thorns stands for**

26 **those who hear, but as they go on their way they are**

27 **choked by life's worries, riches, and pleasures, and they**

28 **do not mature. But the seed on good soil stands for those**

29 **with a noble and good heart, who hear the Word of God,**

30 **retain it, and by persevering produce a crop.** [2]

31

32

33

34

35 [2] *Luke 8:11-15*

On Location! With Brock Tully

THEME: Palm Sunday.

SCRIPTURE: **Matthew 21:1-11** — The triumphal entry of Jesus into Jerusalem.

SYNOPSIS: An interviewer talks to people to find out the little but significant details behind Jesus' entry into Jerusalem.

CHARACTERS: Brock Tully — TV interviewer
3 persons to be interviewed
Gil — Announcer (Off-stage voice)

COSTUMES: Contemporary clothes. Trenchcoat for Brock.

PROPS: Microphone

SETTING: Jerusalem. Place three chairs off to one side for the three persons being interviewed.

1   *(Scene opens with BROCK standing at the front holding a*
2   *microphone. The people he interviews should all be sitting*
3   *together and stand when interviewed.)*
4   GIL: *(From Off-stage)* **And now we take you on location in the**
5   **Holy City with Brock Tully. Over to you, Brock.**
6   BROCK: **Thanks, Gil. I am here in Jerusalem covering the**
7   **Passover which is just getting started. As you can see**
8   **behind me, the city is just packed with people. They have**
9   **come from all over the country for this most important**
10   **holiday, Passover. The crowd here is still pretty excited**
11   **because we just had a parade. A teacher and self-styled**
12   **prophet of sorts named Jesus Bar Joseph just came into**
13   **the city. It was really rather extraordinary. He rode in**
14   **on a donkey, quite humbly and low-key, but immediately**
15   **the people threw palm branches and their coats to the**
16   **ground, carpeting his path. They cheered and whistled**
17   **and shouted, "Hosanna, Hosanna!"; which literally means**
18   **"Save us." Some people think he is, or will be some kind**
19   **of king.** *(BROCK approaches PERSON #1.)* **Excuse me, do**
20   **you think this Jesus is a king?**
21   PERSON #1:   *(Stands and speaks confidently.)* **Yes.**
22   BROCK: **Can you tell us why?**
23   PERSON #1:   **Because Jesus said he was.**
24   BROCK: **Hmmm . . . is there any significance to the donkey?**
25   PERSON #1:   **Yes, there is. A king on a horse means war, but**
26   **a king on a donkey means peace.**
27   BROCK: **So if Jesus is to be king, he wants to be a king of**
28   **peace. That could be tough in a country that is ruled by**
29   **the Romans! There's not room for any king besides**
30   **Caesar.** *(PERSON #1 sits. BROCK turns to PERSON #2.)*
31   **What about the palm branches?**
32   PERSON #2:   *(Stands.)* **Oftentimes when a king returns from a**
33   **war that he won, we will give him a big welcome with**
34   **palm branches, and sometimes we throw our coats down,**
35   **too.**

1   BROCK: Do *you* think Jesus is a king?
2   PERSON #2: I think he's a nice guy who's misguided.
3   *(PERSON #2 sits.)*
4   BROCK: *(To PERSON #3)* How about you, do you think Jesus
5   is a king?
6   PERSON #3: *(Stands.)* I think he might become one. The
7   people were pretty excited today. We're behind him.
8   BROCK: What about the Romans?
9   PERSON #3: I'm pretty sick of the Romans! A lot of us are
10   ready for a change. Who knows, maybe this Jesus is the
11   Messiah. I think we're ready to fight and help him become
12   king. *(PERSON #3 sits. BROCK turns back toward the*
13   *congregation.)*
14   BROCK: There you have it, Gil. The people are looking for
15   someone to free them from Roman control, and they seem
16   very supportive of Jesus. However, by riding into
17   Jerusalem on a donkey, Jesus is making a definite
18   statement that if he is a king, then he is a king of peace.
19   Jesus has made a grand entry into the city — an
20   entry full of symbolism. The Romans will most definitely
21   be watching him. Support among his own people seems
22   very high. Jesus will certainly be the interesting one to
23   observe this week.
24   This is Brock Tully at the Passover in Jerusalem.
25   Back to you, Gil. *(Freeze)*
26
27
28
29
30
31
32
33
34
35

On the Beach

THEME: Forgiveness.

SCRIPTURE: **I John 1:9** — "If we confess our sins, he is faithful and just and will forgive us our sins, and purify us from all unrighteousness."
Psalm 103:12 — "As far as the east is from the west, so far has he removed our transgressions from us."

SYNOPSIS: Two fathers take their kids to the beach for the day. One man has trouble believing that God really forgives and forgets.

CHARACTERS: Neil
Ross
(Two dads)

COSTUMES: Casual "bumming around" clothes.

PROPS: A sand pail and shovel.

SETTING: The beach. Set two lawn chairs Center Stage.

"Ally, take the bucket off Nathan's head. Thank you, sweetheart."

1 *(Scene opens with NEIL and ROSS walking On-stage carrying*
2 *the lawn chairs and the sand pail with a shovel in it. They set*
3 *up and get comfortable as they talk. The ocean or lake should*
4 *be in front of them so that all lines to the kids are directed forward*
5 *toward the audience. Many of the lines are interrupted. Timing*
6 *is critical here for the humor to work.)*
7 **ROSS:** *(Looking toward the congregation, yelling)* **I said, "I've got**
8 **your sand pail and shovel. If you want it . . ."** *(Pause like*
9 *the child is talking back.)* **I said . . . I said,** *(Emphatically)*
10 **Nathan, I said, "I've got your sand pail and shovel. If you**
11 **want it, you'll have to come up here and get it."** *(Pause)*
12 **That's right, it's right here in my hand.** *(Holds it up.)* **No,**
13 **Neil won't use it.** *(Turns to NEIL, in a normal volume.)* **You**
14 **aren't planning on using these, are you, Neil?**
15 **NEIL:** **Not right away, anyway.**
16 **ROSS:** **Say, Neil, I have . . .**
17 **NEIL:** *(Notices his daughter and cuts ROSS off.)* **Ally! Ally!**
18 **Please don't put that sand on Nathan's neck . . . yes, that's**
19 **right, honey. Yeah, and take the bucket off of his head.**
20 **There you go.** *(To ROSS)* **She just loves Nathan.**

1   ROSS: *(Dryly)* **I can see that.** *(They both plop into the lawn chairs.)*
2   **Whoa, this feels great.**
3   NEIL: **You're telling me. Why, I haven't been out in the sun**
4   **like this for** *(Looks at his watch)* **probably three or four**
5   **hours.**
6   ROSS: **Yeah? Well, I work inside all day, so this is a real treat**
7   **for me.** *(Pause as they enjoy the sun.)* **Neil, I've been**
8   **wondering** . . . *(Notices Nathan on the beach, sits up and yells.)*
9   **Nathan, don't put those shells in Ally's swimsuit.** *(A beat)*
10   **Because it's not polite, that's why.**
11   NEIL: **It's not polite?**
12   ROSS: **Well, I couldn't think of a good reason why he**
13   **shouldn't do something that I do to his mother all the**
14   **time.** *(Pause)* **Say, Neil, as I've** . . .
15   NEIL: *(Cuts him off.)* **Ally, take the bucket off of Nathan's head** . . .
16   **Thank you, Sweetheart. I tell you, Ross, she's crazy about**
17   **your son.**
18   ROSS: *(Determined to say what's on his mind)* **Neil, you know Liz**
19   **and I have really worked things out and she's forgiven**
20   **me for, well** . . . **you know, for all the stuff I did.**
21   NEIL: **You're lucky to have a wife like Liz.**
22   ROSS: **I know. Well, like I said, she's forgiven me, but Neil,**
23   **it's hard for me to believe that God has forgiven me.**
24   NEIL: *(Suddenly serious)* **Ross, have you asked God for**
25   **forgiveness?**
26   ROSS: **Yes, I have.**
27   NEIL: *(Relaxing)* **Then it's a done deal.**
28   ROSS: *(Shaking his head slowly)* **That just seems too simple. I**
29   *am* **sorry, and I** *did* **pray for forgiveness. But it seems**
30   **like there should be more.**
31   NEIL: **God says that if we tell him our sin, he will be faithful**
32   **to forgive us. It's that simple. It's still pretty amazing,**
33   **though, that he does forgive us.**
34   ROSS: *(Earnestly)* **But don't you think he remembers what**
35   **we've done wrong? And, if he remembers, how could he**

1   **completely forgive me?**
2   **NEIL:** *(Sits up and looks out.)* **You see how the kids are writing**
3   **in the sand with the sticks?**
4   **ROSS:**   Yeah, only Ally is poking Nathan with her stick.
5   **NEIL:** *(Shrugs.)* **Well, she's nuts about him. Now watch. Every**
6   **now and then a big wave comes in and washes away all**
7   **the marks that the kids have made in the sand.**
8   **Like . . . now. See how the wave washed Nathan's pictures**
9   **away?**
10   **ROSS:**   Yeah, so?
11   **NEIL:**   That's how God deals with our sin. It's like every time
12   we do something wrong, a record of it is written in the
13   sand. When we ask for forgiveness, God sends a big wave
14   in to wash it all away. And then it's gone forever. *(Slowly,*
15   *for emphasis)* **It's like there was never anything there in**
16   **the first place.**
17   **ROSS:** **Wow.** *(Shakes his head slowly up and down in*
18   *understanding.)* **That makes a lot of sense. Neil, that helps**
19   **a lot. Thanks.**
20   **NEIL:** *(Ruefully)* **Well, Ross, I've been there myself, many**
21   **times. God is always faithful to forgive when we are truly**
22   **sorry.** *(Suddenly ROSS and NEIL look out at the "lake" with*
23   *distressed expressions. They immediately stand up and yell to*
24   *their kids.)* **Ally!**
25   **ROSS:**   **Nathan!**
26   **NEIL and ROSS:**   **Put your swimsuits back on, kids!** *(They take*
27   *one step forward as if going after the kids and freeze.)*
28
29
30
31
32
33
34
35

The Outboard Motor

THEME: **The Holy Spirit** — The Spirit is our power for living the life that God has called us to.

SCRIPTURE: **Acts 1:8** — "But you will receive power when the Holy Spirit comes on you . . ."
John 16:5-15 — The coming of the Holy Spirit.

SYNOPSIS: A man, who has been rowing his speed boat, finds out that what he thought was an anchor is actually an outboard motor. This skit shows how the Holy Spirit, who is often ignored, is our power for living.

CHARACTERS: Vern — boat owner
Burt — friend
Narrator

COSTUMES: Casual clothes.

PROPS: None.

SETTING: Vern's driveway.

"Let me get this straight. You say that you have been rowing this boat?"

1 (*Scene opens with VERN miming that he is washing down his*
2 *boat.*)
3 NARRATOR: The Holy Spirit is a person with his own
4 personality. It is he that can infuse us with power and
5 transform our daily lives. However, we are often not
6 aware of all that he can do.
7 VERN: (*Straightening up*) Oh boy, is my back sore, and my
8 arms feel like they're gonna fall off. This boat has turned
9 out to be a big disappointment. Why, it doesn't even have
10 a good anchor.
11 BURT: Hi, Vern. What are you up to? Say! Where did you get
12 this boat? What a beaut!
13 VERN: Oh you know, it's just something I picked up ...
14 BURT: Well, this boat looks like it could go awfully fast!
15 VERN: That's what I thought when I bought it, but so far it's
16 been a big disappointment.
17 BURT: Yeah? How so?
18 VERN: Well, it's so big that I can't row it by myself; I have to
19 get my wife to help me. Even then, we don't get going
20 very fast and my arms still get mighty sore! What a

1   disappointment . . .

2   BURT: Let me get this straight. You say that you have been

3   rowing this boat?

4   VERN: Yes. What else could we do?

5   BURT: Vern, what about the motor?

6   VERN: What motor?

7   BURT: The outboard motor at the back of this boat.

8   VERN: *(Pause)* Is that what that is? I thought it was an

9   anchor. I kept throwing it in when we wanted to fish. It

10   was a disappointment as an anchor, I can tell you that much!

11   BURT: Vern, this boat came with all the power you could

12   ever want. Yet because you didn't know it was there, it

13   was useless to you. Now what are you going to do?

14   VERN: I'm gonna buy me a real anchor. What a

15   disappointment. *(Freeze)*

16   NARRATOR: Sometimes we are like Vern. We have the

17   power of the Holy Spirit available to us, but because we

18   don't recognize it, nothing happens. The Holy Spirit is

19   the living presence of Jesus Christ inside of us. He can

20   be our power for living if we let him.

21

22

23

24

25

26

27

28

29

30

31

32

33

34

35

The Phone Call

THEME: The Second Coming of Christ.

SCRIPTURE: Matthew 24 — Jesus' prophecy on his return.

SYNOPSIS: A couple awaits a phone call from their daughter who ran away from home. She has written a letter telling them that she will call when she gets into town and if they don't answer the phone, she will take that to mean that they don't want her back.

CHARACTERS: Jeff
Linda
(Husband and wife)

COSTUMES: Regular clothing.

PROPS: Telephone

SOUND EFFECTS: Tape of a phone ringing about five times.

SETTING: Jeff and Linda's living room. Place a stool or high table Center Stage to place the telephone on.

1 *(Scene opens with JEFF pacing the room and LINDA standing*
2 *beside the phone, biting her nails.)*
3 LINDA: *(Frustrated)* **Ring, ring, you dumb phone!**
4 JEFF: **Yelling at it is not going to help. Just relax, Linda. If**
5 **she's going to call, she'll call. There's nothing we can do**
6 **to make it happen.**
7 LINDA: **But it's almost dark outside and she said she would**
8 **call** *today.*
9 JEFF: **Who knows what she meant by that? She can't expect**
10 **us to spend the whole day within earshot of the phone.**
11 **Who does she think she is, dictating to us how we should**
12 **live?**
13 LINDA: **All she asked is that we be ready. Is that too much?**
14 JEFF: **It is when I don't really think she's going to call.**
15 LINDA: **Don't say that. Oh, please don't say that.** *(Sits down*
16 *beside the phone.)* **Ever since she left I have prayed that**
17 **she would come back, that she would at least call or send**
18 **a card to say that she was OK.**
19 JEFF: **So your prayers were answered — she sent a letter,**
20 **she's OK. Be satisfied with that.**
21 LINDA: *(Standing up and coming over to him)* **But she said she**
22 **would come through town today and that she'd call, and**
23 **if we wanted her back we were to answer the phone and**
24 *say so,* **but if we didn't answer the phone, she would keep**
25 **on traveling.**
26 JEFF: **So she changed her mind, or maybe she never was**
27 **coming through town.**
28 LINDA: *(Denial)* **No, no.**
29 JEFF: **She made it all up. It probably sounded so romantic to**
30 **her at the time. I'll tell you one thing, though, you can't**
31 **live your life in a constant state of expectation. You can't**
32 **spend the rest of the day just hanging around, and**
33 **waiting for the phone to ring.**
34 LINDA: *(Defiantly)* **And why not?**
35 JEFF: **Because after two years of silence, it doesn't make**

1   sense that all of a sudden she's interested in coming back.

2 LINDA: *(Rising intensity)* **But I have a letter saying that she**

3   **will call sometime today.**

4 JEFF: **And today is almost over! Face it, Linda, it's not going**

5   **to ring.**

6 LINDA: *(Desperate)* **She said she is coming back.**

7 JEFF: **So she lied.**

8 LINDA: **How can you say that? Don't you want her back?**

9   **She's your daughter too.**

10 JEFF: *(Bitter)* **She ran away.**

11 LINDA: **But now she's coming home, just like she promised.**

12   *(Faltering)* **Isn't she?**

13 JEFF: **Linda,** *(Puts his arm around her)* **it's getting late. She**

14   **may have had the best intentions in the world, but if she**

15   **hasn't called by now, I don't think she will.**

16 LINDA: *(Broken)* **But Jeff . . .**

17 JEFF: **I'll tell you what — let's run downtown and get some**

18   **dinner. We haven't been out of the house all day.**

19 LINDA: **But the phone . . .**

20 JEFF: **It's not going to ring, Linda.** *(JEFF takes LINDA by the*

21   *arm and guides her Off-stage and out of sight of the congregation.*

22   *As soon as they are gone, the phone begins to ring. It should ring*

23   *four or five times for maximum effect.)*

24

25

26

27

28

29

30

31

32

33

34

35

Phone Calls to Home

THEME: **Hypocrisy** — Unless the things we do line up with the good things we say, we are like the Pharisees.

SCRIPTURE: **Luke 18:9-14** — The parable of the tax collector and the Pharisee.

SYNOPSIS: Three ladies are making phone calls to their homes from adjacent pay phones. From the different responses of the first two ladies to the third, we come to understand how words are empty if our actions belie them.

CHARACTERS: Julie — emotional and distraught, her life is a mess
Ann — legalistic and proud, very businesslike
Sandy — trying her best to be a Christian but quite discouraged

COSTUMES: Regular attire.

PROPS: None.

SETTING: A shopping mall.

"Hi, honey, I'm at the mall."

1   *(Scene opens with all three ladies in the process of placing their*
2   *phone calls. JULIE should be in the middle. They should stand*
3   *in a straight line about two feet apart. Each one should*
4   *pantomime holding a phone. When the sketch starts, all three*
5   *should put the money in their phones and dial . . . The lines need*
6   *to go fast with each actor cutting off the line of the preceding*
7   *actor. When they are not speaking, they should look as if they*
8   *are listening to whomever is on the end of their phone lines.)*
9   **SANDY:**   **Hi, Nick, how are you doing?**
10   **ANN:**   **Hi, honey, I'm at the mall.**
11   **JULIE:**   *(Hopefully)* **Bob? Thank heavens you're still here.**
12   **SANDY:**   **I'm down here at the mall.** *(Pause)* **No, it hasn't been**
13   **a very good day.**
14   **ANN:**   **Yes, I met with Clara.** *(Pause)* **I think it went fine,**
15   **although I'm sure she doesn't feel that way!**
16   **SANDY:**   **I lost my temper again with Shirley. I feel terrible.**
17   **JULIE:**   **Bob . . . does this mean that you are going to stay**
18   **after all?**
19   **ANN:**   **Of course I was hard on her! There is such a thing as**
20   **righteous anger, you know. Clara has to learn that if she**

1 is going to use the Sunday school class before me, she
2 will have to clean it up. Godliness is next to tidiness. I
3 think it says that somewhere in Proverbs.
4 SANDY: Yeah ... I know. When I calmed down, I asked for
5 her forgiveness, but I just keep thinking, "I'm a poor
6 excuse for a Christian."
7 JULIE: *(A catch in her voice, a little louder)* Please, please, Bob,
8 I'll do anything ...
9 ANN: *(Gives JULIE a dirty look.)* I don't care if Clara has taught
10 Sunday school for thirty-five years! If she can't be neat,
11 she must need spiritual healing somewhere in her life.
12 SANDY: I just want God to use me, but I feel like I blow it so
13 often.
14 ANN: Well, maybe so, but I am just thankful that God has
15 worked in my life, molding me and using me as a
16 tremendous instrument of his holy will.
17 JULIE: *(Loudly and in anguish)* Bob!
18 ANN: *(Darkly to JULIE)* Shhh ...
19 SANDY: Oh, oh, I think the lady on the phone beside me is in
20 some kind of trouble.
21 JULIE: *(Crying out)* No, no, don't leave me!
22 ANN: *(Hand over the receiver)* Get a grip, young lady, you are
23 being rude! There are other people using the phone too!
24 *(Into the phone)* The lady beside me is going off the deep
25 end, I think.
26 SANDY: I gotta go. This lady beside me needs some kind of
27 help ... I'll see you at home ... Love you too. *(She hangs
28 up the phone quickly and turns to JULIE, putting her arm around
29 her. JULIE is standing with the phone in her hand, her arm
30 hanging limp.)*
31 JULIE: *(Dully)* He left me. *(A loud cry)* He left me!
32 ANN: *(Coldly)* Can you please fix your life elsewhere? I am
33 trying to talk on the phone. *(Freeze)*
34
35

Raising a Dad

THEME: **Conformity** — Peer pressure and a desire to fit in and be liked can cause us to conform to this world, no matter what our ages.

SCRIPTURE: **Romans 12:2** — "Do not conform any longer to the pattern of this world, but be transformed by the renewing of your mind."

SYNOPSIS: Two teenage girls share their frustration in trying to raise their fathers to be good Christian men. The point is made that we all struggle, no matter what our age, with conforming to the mold of the world.

CHARACTERS: Lindsey
Jessica
(Two high school girls)

COSTUMES: Regular clothes.

PROPS: Two cups and saucers.

SETTING: Lindsey's kitchen. Place a table and two chairs Center Stage.

1　　*(Scene opens with LINDSEY and JESSICA laughing and*
2　　*drinking coffee. The scene should be reminiscent of two mothers*
3　　*having coffee together.)*
4　LINDSEY:　*(Laughing)* **I know what you mean. It's bad**
5　　**enough trying to finish high school, let alone raise two**
6　　**parents by myself!**
7　JESSICA:　**Raise your parents? Now that's another whole**
8　　**topic.**
9　LINDSEY:　**Tell me about it! This has been quite the week**
10　　**with Dad. Sometimes I don't think he'll ever grow up**
11　　**right. How has it been going with your dad?**
12　JESSICA:　**My Steve is doing OK. I worry about him, though.**
13　LINDSEY:　**In what way?**
14　JESSICA:　**Well, he is so susceptible to peer pressure.**
15　LINDSEY:　*(Shaking her head)* **Aren't they all?**
16　JESSICA:　**He always wants to dress just like his friends —**
17　　**all he ever wears is a suit and a tie.**
18　LINDSEY:　**I know. I went down to Dad's office one day. They**
19　　**all look the same.**
20　JESSICA:　**He's afraid that they won't like him if he looks**
21　　**different. He thinks that if he doesn't dress up, they won't**
22　　**want him to work there.**
23　LINDSEY:　**I'd say if they only hired him because of his**
24　　**clothes, then he needs to find a new job.**
25　JESSICA:　**Exactly! But can he understand that?**
26　LINDSEY and JESSICA:　*(Together)* **Nooo . . .**
27　LINDSEY:　**Well, my Larry listens to the worst music.**
28　JESSICA:　**Oh, don't get me started on that!**
29　LINDSEY:　**It's all that old stuff from the fifties and sixties! I**
30　　**don't think he even liked it when it first came out, but**
31　　**all his friends listen to it, so . . .**
32　JESSICA:　**Lindsey, I know what you mean. I'm always telling**
33　　**my Steve, "Dad, if all your friends jumped off a bridge,**
34　　**would you do it too?"**
35　LINDSEY:　**What does he say to that?**

1 **LINDSEY and JESSICA:** *(Together whining)* **But this is**
2 **different.**
3 **JESSICA:** I guess what worries me the most is that he doesn't
4 seem all that different from his friends. I really want him
5 to grow up to be a fine Christian man, but his goals and
6 dreams seem to be the same as his friends that don't
7 believe.
8 **LINDSEY:** That's tough. There is such pressure to conform
9 out there.
10 **JESSICA:** He's a good guy and his heart is in the right place,
11 but I'm afraid that he is buying into a definition of success
12 that has nothing to do with living a life for God.
13 **LINDSEY:** He'll just have to discover that on his own,
14 Jessica.
15 **JESSICA:** I know. *(Sigh)* You can't live their lives for them.
16 **LINDSEY:** And you can't tell them anything, either. They
17 always have to do it their way. Even if it is harder.
18 **JESSICA:** *(Nods in agreement and then looks at her watch.)* **Well,**
19 **I should go. Thanks for the listening ear.**
20 **LINDSEY:** No problem-o. I'll see you at school tomorrow.
21 *(Calls after JESSICA as she leaves.)* **And if you figure out a**
22 **way to get our dads to keep their hair shorter, let me**
23 **know.** *(Freeze)*
24
25
26
27
28
29
30
31
32
33
34
35

A Reflection

THEME: Love.

SCRIPTURE: **John 13:34, 35** — "A new commandment I give you: Love one another. As I have loved you, so you must love one another. By this all men will know that you are my disciples, if you love one another."

SYNOPSIS: Two friends share their frustrations with sharing their faith. They realize that if they can reflect God's love, like the moon reflects the sun's light, their friends will see God in them.

CHARACTERS: Robin
Andy
(Two students, male or female)

COSTUMES: School clothes.

PROPS: Notebook, pen, globe, and a flashlight.

SETTING: School. Set a stool Center Stage to hold the globe.

"Don't you think she'd listen to what you have to say?"

1 (Scene opens with ANDY shining a flashlight on the globe. The
2 flashlight should be aimed at Egypt. ROBIN, who is holding the
3 notebook and a pen, is crouched down on the other side of the
4 globe trying to see what is directly across from Egypt on the globe.)
5 **ANDY:** It's the hottest day of the year in Cairo, Egypt — one
6 hundred and forty-nine degrees in the shade. People are
7 literally exploding from the heat. But the big question
8 is, if it's the middle of the day in Cairo, where would it
9 be the middle of the night?
10 **ROBIN:** *(Squinting at the underside of the globe)* **L.A. It's the**
11 **middle of the night in Los Angeles.** *(Straightens up and*
12 *writes that in her notebook.)* **Just one more. It is day in Sri**
13 **Lanka. What would it be in Sydney, Australia?**
14 **ANDY:** *(Spins the globe trying to find Sri Lanka.)* **I talked to**
15 **Karen today.**
16 **ROBIN:** *(Searching the globe as well)* **Yeah? How did it go?**
17 **ANDY:** Not so hot. I really want her to know that I've become
18 a believer but I'm afraid if I tell her, she'll just laugh.
19 **ROBIN:** Why would she laugh?
20 **ANDY:** Because I'm not that much different now from who I

1   used to be.
2   ROBIN: I think you've changed a lot. She's your friend. Don't
3   you think she'd listen to what you have to say?
4   ANDY: It's got to be more than words. I want her to
5   understand that God loves her, but to tell her isn't
6   enough. Somehow she's got to *see* it.
7   ROBIN: *(Looking up at ANDY)* If you love her, Andy, then she'll
8   start to see God's love.
9   ANDY: How do you figure that?
10 ROBIN: I think that God works through us. It's kind of like
11   we're his arms and feet. We do and say what he needs
12   done and said. If we love people, people will see that we
13   know God because love comes from God.
14 ANDY: But she'll just think that it's my love.
15 ROBIN: *(Shaking head)* No, Karen will know your love is
16   something different, because we reflect God's love.
17 ANDY: Reflect? This is starting to sound pretty complicated,
18   Robin.
19 ROBIN: Look, shine the flashlight again. See how it's dark on
20   this side of the globe? But if the moon is out, like my
21   hand here, *(Balls up fist and holds it away from the globe like*
22   *the moon)* it reflects the sun's light onto the earth at night.
23   We can reflect God's love. People see and know us, but
24   the love we have is a reflection of God's love.
25 ANDY: So, God works through us.
26 ROBIN: That's right. He loves us and, in turn, we love other
27   people.
28 ANDY: This could be a lot more simple than trying to think
29   of all the right words to tell Karen about God's love. I'll
30   try and reflect his love to her.
31 ROBIN: *(Looking back at the globe)* So, have you found Sri Lanka?
32 ANDY: I sure have. *(Puts his finger on Sri Lanka.)* Where is the
33   moon shining if the sun is up in Sri Lanka?
34 ROBIN: *(Looks at the globe and then up at ANDY.)* Japan. *(Freeze)*
35

Rick and the Socks

THEME: **Stewardship** — Stewardship is not being responsible with what *we* own, but it is being responsible with what *God* has given us.

SCRIPTURE: **Job 41:11** — "Everything under heaven belongs to [God]."
I Corinthians 4:2 — "Those who have been given a trust must prove faithful."

SYNOPSIS: On his dad's birthday, Rick neglects to buy a present because he has spent all his money on himself. Rick's mother points out that all Rick's money has come from his dad in the form of allowances. She makes the point that Rick's father is willing to keep giving him money and the least Rick can do is give a part back in the form of a birthday present. As Christians, our stewardship lies not in being responsible with what we own, but rather in being responsible with what God has given us.

CHARACTERS: Mom
Dad
Rick, their son
Narrator

COSTUMES: Regular attire.

PROPS: Several pairs of socks, gift wrap, one gift-wrapped box of socks.

SETTING: Dad's birthday celebration in the living room. Set up four chairs — one for each member of the family and one to hold a pile of socks (Dad should sit beside the chair with the socks). Crumpled gift wrap should be strewn about.

1   *(Scene opens with DAD opening one last present.)*

2   **DAD:**   Socks! Thanks a lot, dear. How thoughtful of you. *(He*

3   *puts the socks on the pile of socks in front of him.)*

4   **MOM:**   You're welcome, honey. Happy birthday.

5   **RICK:**   Yeah, happy birthday, Dad. *(MOM and DAD stare at*

6   *RICK.)* **What?**

7   **MOM:**   Well, don't you have anything to give your father?

8   **RICK:**   But I don't have any money.

9   **DAD:**   Rick, I gave you twenty dollars on Friday for your

10   allowance.

11   **RICK:**   But, Dad, I have such a high overhead! That mountain

12   bike you bought me is so *cheap* that I'm always buying

13   new parts!

14   **DAD:**   *(Sigh)* Son, I don't think you understand . . . Well, I

15   should get to the yard work I was going to do today. *(DAD*

16   *exits.)*

17   **RICK:**   What's the matter with him?

18   **MOM:**   Well, he would never say it, but I think he's

19   disappointed that you never gave him a present.

20   **RICK:**   But he has all kinds of stuff, and you and Dad have a

21   lot of money. What could I possibly give him that he could

22   need?

23   **MOM:**   Rick, the point isn't whether or not he needs anything,

24   it's whether you care enough about your father to show

25   him with a gift.

26   **RICK:**   Well, it's my money and I've spent it.

27   **MOM:**   *(A little upset)* But it's *not* your money.

28   **RICK:**   Hey, Mom, I mowed the lawn, did the dishes twice and

29   took the garbage halfway out. I earned that money! I

30   know kids who do less and get paid more!

31   **MOM:**   *(Softly)* And I know kids who don't get any allowance

32   at all. Some parents just don't have any money to give

33   to their children. We don't have to give you an allowance,

34   but we want you to have it.

35   **RICK:**   And I can do with it as I want. Right?

1 MOM: Sure, but I think a little gratitude is in order.
2   Everything you have was either given to you by your
3   father and me, or else you bought it with money we gave
4   you.
5 RICK: *(Realization dawning)* So, really, everything I have
6   actually belongs to you and Dad.
7 MOM: That's right. But we want you to have those things.
8   We love you.
9 RICK: But if Dad can give me twenty bucks every week, at
10   least I could give him back a five-dollar present.
11 MOM: That's right, Rick. You know, I wouldn't have made
12   such a big deal out of this, but *my* birthday is coming up
13   next month. Well, I think I'll check on your father. *(Gathers*
14   *up socks and leaves.)*
15 RICK: *(Reflectively)* Hmmm . . . Mom is right. The least I can do
16   is give back to Dad part of what he gave me. I really
17   should go out and get him a birthday present. *(Yells.)* Say,
18   Mom, what is Dad's sock size? *(Freeze)*
19 NARRATOR: Good stewardship is not being responsible
20   with what *we* own, but with what God has so graciously
21   allowed us to have.
22
23
24
25
26
27
28
29
30
31
32
33
34
35

The Road Trip

THEME: The Bible — The answers to many of the questions we have lie in God's message to us: the Bible.

SCRIPTURE: Micah 6:8 — "He has showed you, O man, what is good. And what does the Lord require of you? To act justly and to love mercy and to walk humbly with your God."

SYNOPSIS: A couple gets lost while on a road trip, but the man refuses to consult a map. This scene parallels our own stubbornness to look to God's guidelines for living — the Bible — when we are lost.

CHARACTERS: Neil — Confident and stubborn
Sharol — A worrier but right in her perceptions of things
Narrator

COSTUMES: Casual clothes.

PROPS: Jacket, Bible.

SETTING: A car. Place two chairs side by side Center Stage.

"We are totally lost. Why can't you admit it?"

1   *(Scene opens with NEIL and SHAROL miming riding in a car.*
2   *NEIL should have an intense look on his face as he drives. He*
3   *should never look at her as he talks but should be completely*
4   *absorbed in what he is doing. SHAROL should be chewing her*
5   *lip and looking worried.)*
6   **SHAROL:** *(Tentatively)* **Don't you think you're driving just a**
7   **little too fast, Neil?**
8   **NEIL:** *(Irritated)* **No, I don't think that. We're already late as**
9   **it is.**
10   **SHAROL:** **Grandma won't mind if we're a little late to the**
11   **reunion just as long as we do get there sometime this**
12   **weekend** *(To herself)* **and as long as we arrive alive.**
13   **NEIL:** **Sharol, why don't you look at the mountains and just**
14   **relax?**
15   **SHAROL:** *(Hesitantly)* **Well, Neil, that's another thing that**
16   **worries me a bit. I don't remember there being mountains**
17   **between Fort Collins and Iowa.**
18   **NEIL:** *(Tersely)* **What are you trying to say?**
19   **SHAROL:** **I think you should look at a map.**
20   **NEIL:** **I don't need a map. I know** *exactly* **where I am going.**

1   SHAROL: I know exactly where we are going too — I just
2   think you don't know how to get there. Let's pull over
3   and ask for directions.
4   NEIL: *(Panicky)* No! We can't do that!
5   SHAROL: Why not?
6   NEIL: What if someone recognizes me and sees me asking for
7   directions? I don't think I could ever live that down.
8   SHAROL: OK, let *me* look at the map then.
9   NEIL: *(Recovering)* No. We don't need a map.
10   SHAROL: Why not?
11   NEIL: *(Thinking fast)* Because . . . I have it completely
12   memorized. Yeah, that's it.
13   SHAROL: Give me a break, you have it completely
14   memorized?
15   NEIL: Yes, I did it when I turned thirteen. It was part of
16   becoming a man in my family.
17   SHAROL: *(Losing it)* We are totally lost. Why can't you admit
18   it? The map *(Waves it in front of his face)* has the answers
19   to the questions you are too stubborn to ask. Neil, to use
20   a map is not a sign of weakness.
21   NEIL: Now hold on a minute, Sharol. I have my pride, you
22   know.
23   SHAROL: What good is your pride if we end up in Arizona
24   instead of at Grandma's in Iowa? You will have done it
25   on your own, all right, but big deal, *we would still be in*
26   *the wrong place.* *(NEIL mimes putting on the blinkers and*
27   *pulling over.)* Hey, what are you doing?
28   NEIL: What does it look like? I'm stopping at this gas station.
29   *(He puts a blanket/jacket over his head and crouches down on*
30   *the seat.)* Go out there, will you, and ask somebody for
31   directions. *(Freeze)*
32   NARRATOR: Oftentimes we are like Neil; we are too
33   stubborn to admit that we are misguided or lost. And we
34   are too proud to look to our map *(Holds up a Bible)* and
35   use the directions that we know are there.

The Salesclerk

THEME: **Spiritual knowledge** — To represent the faith well, we must know what we believe.

SCRIPTURE: **Titus 1:9** — "Hold firmly to the trustworthy message as it has been taught ... encourage others by sound doctrine and refute those who oppose it."

SYNOPSIS: A man trying to buy his wife a gift finds the salesclerk rather uninformed and a poor representative of the store. As Christians, we must know what we believe to be good representatives of our faith.

CHARACTERS: Salesclerk — overly confident
Husband
Narrator

COSTUMES: Salesclerk should be dressed up fashionably.

PROPS: None.

SETTING: Ladies department of a clothing store. The racks and clothes are implied by pantomime.

1   *(Scene opens with the SALESCLERK miming straightening*
2   *things up. HUSBAND wanders in and starts browsing.)*
3   **HUSBAND: Boy, I don't even know where to begin. Well, I**
4   **guess I do know that I have to buy something . . . Hmmm**
5   **. . . this doesn't look too bad.**
6   **SALESCLERK: Can I help you, sir?**
7   **HUSBAND:** *(Sigh)* **I hope so. I'm looking for a birthday gift**
8   **for my wife, and I really don't know where to start.**
9   **SALESCLERK:** *(Mimes pulling a dress off of a rack.)* **Well, how**
10   **about this dress? This color would look lovely on your**
11   **wife.**
12   **HUSBAND: How can you say that? You've never even met my**
13   **wife.**
14   **SALESCLERK:** *(Unfazed)* **Well, this is a lovely dress, and I**
15   **am sure that your wife is a lovely woman. Lovely goes**
16   **with lovely, I've always said.**
17   **HUSBAND: Uh . . . I think I'll just look around a bit on my**
18   **own, thanks.** *(He takes a couple of steps and starts looking at*
19   *another rack.)*
20   **SALESCLERK:** *(Calls over.)* **Everything on that rack is twenty**
21   **dollars.**
22   **HUSBAND:** *(To himself)* **Then how come the sign says**
23   **"Various prices from thirty to fifty dollars?"**
24   **SALESCLERK: Pardon me?**
25   **HUSBAND: Oh, the sign says that these dresses are priced**
26   **from thirty to fifty dollars.**
27   **SALESCLERK: How do you like that. You take a coffee break**
28   **and they change all the price tags!**
29   **HUSBAND:** *(Back to browsing)* **Say, now this is nice. This is a**
30   **sharp-looking dress. Excuse me, ma'am, do you have this**
31   **in a medium?**
32   **SALESCLERK: This is a medium.**
33   **HUSBAND: No, it's not. Look, see the tag? It has an "S" on it.**
34   **This dress is a small.**
35   **SALESCLERK: Oh, that "S" doesn't mean small, that stands**

1   for "stout."

2 HUSBAND: Stout? No way. "S" means small. It always has.

3 SALESCLERK: *(Sing-songy)* I'm sorry, it means stout. Stout,

4   stout, stout, stout.

5 HUSBAND: I don't believe this. I came in here ready to buy

6   something, but now there is no way I want to spend any

7   money here.

8 SALESCLERK: Why not? Look at all the great clothes we've

9   got.

10 HUSBAND: Says who, you? You don't know anything about

11   the products you sell. You won't admit you're wrong. And

12   you've got all the answers to the questions I haven't even

13   asked!

14 SALESCLERK: Well, I thought you needed help.

15 HUSBAND: Well, so did I, but I guess I didn't. Look, I heard

16   this was a great store, but you really changed my mind.

17   *(He walks out.)*

18 SALESCLERK: *(Calls after him.)* Have a nice day. *(To herself)*

19   Boy, does that guy have an attitude problem.

20 NARRATOR: As believers, it is important that we know what

21   it is we believe. Like the salesclerk, we are often called

22   upon to explain what and who we represent, but unlike

23   the salesclerk, we must be ready to give a sound,

24   knowledgeable defense.

25

26

27

28

29

30

31

32

33

34

35

Salty

THEME: **Evangelism** — It is only by daring to leave our comfort zones that we can make a difference in the world.

SCRIPTURE: **Matthew 5:13** — "You are the salt of the earth."

SYNOPSIS: Grains of salt in a box talk about their purpose in life.

CHARACTERS: Salty — timid and rather afraid person
Merton — gruff, army sergeant type
Rocky — friendly guy

COSTUMES: The three characters can dress all in white.

PROPS: None.

SETTING: Inside a box of salt.

"The next shake and I'm outta here!"

1   *(Scene opens with the "salt" jumping up and down since they*
2   *have just been shaken up. SALTY should be holding on for dear*
3   *life to MERTON.)*
4   **ALL:**   Aaaahhh . . .
5   **SALTY:**   Whew, that was close.
6   **MERTON:**   Would you let go of me?
7   **SALTY:**   I'm sorry. I was scared. Oh no, it looks like they got
8   Whitey.
9   **ROCKY:**   *They* didn't get anyone. Whitey went willingly.
10   **SALTY:**   Weally? I mean really?
11   **ROCKY:**   Sure. It's his job. After all we are salt. And outside
12   this box, somewhere, someday, is where we're supposed
13   to be.
14   **MERTON:**   That's true.
15   **ROCKY:**   Say, I don't think I know you two. Every time they
16   shake the salt shaker sideways, all the salt gets super
17   shook up.
18   **MERTON:**   Salt's the name . . . Merton Salt.
19   **SALTY:**   Salty's my name.
20   **ROCKY:**   My name is Rocky.

1   MERTON: Why were you holding on to me so tightly, Salty?

2   SALTY: Because I don't want to be the salt on someone's

3   meat! I like it here with all the other salt.

4   ROCKY: Say, Salty, since when does a single speck of

5   salt scorn sliding out the sluiceway onto someone's

6   supper?

7   SALTY: I can't help it. I don't want to leave this salt box.

8   This is my home and I am happy here.

9   MERTON: But your job is out there, Salty.

10   ROCKY: If you slyly stay here in secret, you're simply salt

11   to the salt. And there's already plenty of salt here.

12   MERTON: He's right, Salty. Out there you can be a

13   preservative . . .

14   ROCKY: . . . or a superb, succulent seasoning on a sumptuous

15   serving of succotash.

16   MERTON: Out there you can make a difference.

17   SALTY: Really?

18   MERTON: Sure. It's nice to get together and swap salty

19   stories, but out there in the world, on the meat and

20   vegetables, that's where you're really needed.

21   SALTY: I guess I never really thought about being needed.

22   I have a responsibility, don't I? I could make things better.

23   ROCKY: You sure could. A shake of shiny sea salt can spice

24   up a so-so, simple supper.

25   MERTON: And the world will be a tastier place because of

26   you.

27   SALTY: You've convinced me. The next shake and I'm outta

28   here!

29   MERTON: Oh, oh. Here we go! They're shaking the salt

30   shaker again! *(Shake and then freeze.)*

31

32

33

34

35

Service

THEME: **Serving** — One of the ways to find fulfillment as a Christian is to serve others.

SCRIPTURE: **Mark 10:43-45** — "Whoever wants to become great among you must be your servant, and whoever wants to be first must be slave of all. For even the Son of Man did not come to be served, but to serve, and to give his life as a ransom for many."

SYNOPSIS: A comical look at a novice waitress who learns that her job is to serve others. We find fulfillment by serving others. This sketch could also be used in reference to spiritual gifts.

CHARACTERS: Bebe — waitress, dizzy but well-meaning
Rick and Dan — customers
Narrator

COSTUMES: Bebe may wear an apron and name tag.

PROPS: Newspaper or magazine, two glasses, two menus (large folded papers with "MENU" printed on the front).

SETTING: A restaurant. Set up a table and two chairs. If desired, add a tablecloth and flowers. Table should have a jumble of dishes, glasses, etc. on it.

1   *(Scene opens with two customers entering. BEBE is chomping*
2   *on gum and looking bored.)*
3   **RICK:** **Table for two, please.**
4   **BEBE:** **Oh, that's sweet.**
5   **DAN:** **Aren't you supposed to show us where to sit?**
6   **BEBE:** **I don't know. Am I?**
7   **RICK:** **Are you our waitress?**
8   **BEBE:** **Yes, sir! And I want to be the best waitress a person**
9   **can be.**
10   **RICK:** **Well, then, I think it's your job to show us where you**
11   **would like us to sit.**
12   **BEBE:** **Oh. OK. Well, see that little table over there with the**
13   **dirty dishes piled on top of it? You can sit there.**
14   **RICK:** **Thanks . . .**
15   **BEBE:** **Enjoy your meal.** *(RICK and DAN sit down at the table.*
16   *BEBE sits down and starts reading a newspaper or magazine.)*
17   **DAN:** **This place is kind of a mess.**
18   **RICK:** **No kidding! Look at all these dirty dishes.**
19   **DAN:** *(Clears throat a couple of times to get BEBE's attention.)*
20   **Excuse me, Miss . . .**
21   **BEBE:** **Yes?**
22   **DAN:** **Could we have some menus and a couple of glasses of**
23   **water?**
24   **BEBE:** *(Shrugs her shoulders.)* **I don't see why not.** *(Goes back to*
25   *reading her paper.)*
26   **RICK:** *(Shrugs his shoulder, to DAN)* **I think the glasses of water**
27   **are over there.** *(Points Off-stage. DAN exits Off-stage.)*
28   **BEBE:** *(Calling after him)* **Say, while you're over there, could**
29   **you get me a glass of water, too?** *(Sigh)* **This job can be**
30   **so boring! Sometimes there is just nothing to do.** *(DAN*
31   *returns with glasses and menus.)*
32   **DAN:** *(To RICK)* **Here's the water. I found some menus too.**
33   *(Hands RICK menu and glass.)*
34   **RICK:** **Thanks.** *(They look the menus over.)* **Say, uh, we're ready**
35   **to order.**

1 BEBE: So?

2 DAN: So, are you going to come over here and find out
3   what we want to eat?

4 BEBE: Why would I want to know that? Men! They think you
5   want to know every little thing about them!

6 RICK: This is crazy. I'm starting to feel guilty for interrupting
7   her reading.

8 DAN: Hey, come over here for a minute. What's your name?

9 BEBE: Bebe.

10 RICK: Bebe, how long have you been a waitress?

11 BEBE: You mean all the time added up?

12 RICK: Yes.

13 BEBE: Including breaks?

14 RICK: Sure.

15 BEBE: *(Looks at her watch.)* Oh, I'd say about twenty-five
16   minutes.

17 RICK and DAN: *(Together)* Twenty-five minutes!

18 DAN: Well, how do you like your job so far?

19 BEBE: Honestly?

20 RICK and DAN: *(Together)* Honestly!

21 BEBE: Not very much. There isn't enough to do. I don't feel,
22   you know, very fulfilled.

23 RICK: Bebe, do you know what a waitress is supposed to do?

24 BEBE: Well, you should ... First you ... I ... Uh ... I guess
25   I really don't know. Am I not doing a good job?

26 DAN: Bebe, a waitress or waiter *waits* on people who are
27   usually sitting at tables.

28 RICK: You serve people.

29 BEBE: Oooh. *(Chomping gum and looking confused)* So what
30   does that mean?

31 DAN: That means that you show us where to sit.

32 RICK: You give us menus,

33 DAN: and water,

34 RICK: and then you come and take our order.

35 BEBE: So, you don't get *me* a glass of water, I get *you* a glass

137

1   of water.

2   DAN: Exactly.

3   BEBE: Boy, that will really give me something to do with all

4   the time I have. My day will sure go a lot faster.

5   RICK: If you want to be fulfilled and happy as a waitress,

6   you need to serve people; to help.

7   BEBE: Well, I want to be the best waitress I can be! Thanks

8   for your help, guys.

9   DAN: No problem.

10   BEBE: So, can I take your order?

11   RICK: I'm afraid we've got to get back to work.

12   DAN: Good luck, Bebe.

13   BEBE: Thanks. Say, am I supposed to show you to your car?

14   RICK: No, that's fine.

15   BEBE: *(Chasing after RICK and DAN as they head Off-stage)* **Hey**

16   you guys. You forgot to clear your table off!

17   NARRATOR: As Christians, we may find ourselves like the

18   waitress — well meaning, but in the dark as to the nature

19   of our real work. Jesus said, "Whoever wants to become

20   great among you must be your servant, and whoever

21   wants to be first must be slave of all. For even the Son

22   of Man did not come to be served, but to serve, and to

23   give his life as a ransom for many." [1]

24

25

26

27

28

29

30

31

32

33

34

35   [1]*Mark 10:43-45*

Sewing 101

THEME: **Spiritual Knowledge** — It is important to remember the basics of faith. It is the foundation that our lives are built on. And it can make us more effective in our witness for Christ.

SCRIPTURE: **I Peter 3:15** — "Always be prepared to give an answer to everyone who asks you to give the reason for the hope that you have."

SYNOPSIS: Two friends discuss the need to know the basics of their faith. One woman is in a hurry to get a sewing project done, unaware that she has forgotten to thread the needle. When she pulls the project out of the sewing machine, it falls apart.

CHARACTERS: Alice — Frantic but sure of herself, a very cut-and-dried, black-and-white kind of person, a first time seamstress.
Wendy — Christian friend with a good sense of humor.

COSTUMES: Regular attire.

PROPS: One sewing machine (with the thread on top but not threaded through the needle. The end of the thread should hang down in front), some fabric in a bag, a pattern.

SETTING: A sewing room. Set up a table Center Stage to hold the sewing machine and a chair for Alice to sit on as she sews.

1   *(Scene opens with WENDY browsing around the sewing room.*
2   *The sewing machine should be in plain view. ALICE is Off-stage.*
3   *When ALICE comes in, she should sit down, set up and sew all*
4   *the while she is talking.)*
5   **WENDY:** *(Calling Off-stage to ALICE)* **So what did you say to**
6   **him then?**
7   **ALICE:** *(Bustling down the aisle with a bag of fabric in her arms)*
8   **I told him that just because I couldn't explain how Jesus**
9   **could be both God and man, that that didn't mean nobody**
10   **else could.**
11   **WENDY: What did he say to that?**
12   **ALICE: He said that it sounded like I didn't know what I**
13   **believed.**
14   **WENDY: Ouch! That hurts.**
15   **ALICE: Why? I told him that I certainly do know what I**
16   **believe, it's just that I don't know all the details.** *(To*
17   *herself)* **Let's see, I've got the sewing machine, the fabric**
18   **and the pattern. I'm set to go.** *(She folds the material in two*
19   *and proceeds to sew.)*
20   **WENDY: So, do you think that he will ask you about God**
21   **again?**
22   **ALICE:** *(Sigh of exasperation)* **How should I know? I gave him**
23   **the number of the pastor. I said, "This guy is paid to know**
24   **the answers to hard questions. Call him!"**
25   **WENDY:** *(Shaking her head)* **Alice, Alice, Alice. I think you**
26   **may have blown it. It sounds like your friend had some**
27   **serious questions that he needed answered, and** *you* **told**
28   **him to call the pastor.**
29   **ALICE: Nonsense.** *(Sewing furiously)* **You know that God**
30   **always works in spite of us.**
31   **WENDY: But that doesn't give us reason to make God's job**
32   **harder.** *(Noticing ALICE's frantic pace)* **I didn't know you**
33   **knew how to sew, Alice.**
34   **ALICE: Oh, sure, I've been a seamstress now for about** *(Looks*
35   *at her watch)* **ten minutes.**

1   **WENDY:** *(Laughs.)* **What are you making?**

2   **ALICE:** **I promised my daughter a fancy dress for her**

3   **sixteenth birthday,** *(Or for the prom)* **so I decided to sew**

4   **her one.**

5   **WENDY:** **But if you've never sewed before, you should really**

6   **start with something simple and work your way up.**

7   **ALICE:** **Boring . . .** *(Make that long and drawn out.)* **If it looks**

8   **great, who cares about the details?**

9   **WENDY:** **I think that's the point, Alice. It won't look great**

10   **unless you pay attention to the details, and you can only**

11   **do that if you know the basics.**

12   **ALICE:** *(Defensively)* **I'm making it up as I go along.**

13   **WENDY:** **That's what I'm afraid of. Alice, your sewing is like**

14   **your Christian life. If you don't understand the basics**

15   **and know how everything fits together, eventually**

16   **everything will fall apart.**

17   **ALICE:** **Nonense!** *(Pulls out the folded material she has been*

18   *working with.)* **There!**

19   **WENDY:** *(Walks over and gently pulls apart the fabric.)* **You forgot**

20   **to thread the needle.**

21   **ALICE:** *(Brightly)* **I knew that, I was just practicing.**

22   **WENDY:** **Alice, our lives can come apart at the seams if we**

23   **don't know the basics.**

24   **ALICE:** **Time to read the manual?**

25   **WENDY:** **Time to read** *both* **manuals.** *(Freeze)*

26

27

28

29

30

31

32

33

34

35

The Shoe Store

THEME: **The Christian Community** — As Christians, we need each other. Our faith is best lived out and strengthened in the context of community.

SCRIPTURE: **Hebrews 10:25** — "Let us not give up meeting together . . ."

SYNOPSIS: A man who is having trouble with his Christian "walk" thinks he needs a new pair of shoes. The store clerk helps him to see that it is tough to walk alone in our faith. We need the support of other walkers.

CHARACTERS: Bill — customer
Ginger — shoe clerk

COSTUMES: Professional-looking outfit for Ginger.

PROPS: Various pairs of shoes.

SETTING: A shoe store. Set up a table Center Stage to hold the display of shoes.

"Hey, if the shoe fits, wear it."

1　　*(Scene opens with BILL picking up a pair of shoes and looking*
2　　*them over. GINGER enters.)*
3　GINGER:　Hi. Can I help you?
4　BILL:　Uh, yeah. I'm looking for a new pair of shoes.
5　GINGER:　What kind of shoes are you looking for?
6　BILL:　I'm not sure exactly. You see, I've been having some
7　　real trouble with my Christian walk lately, and I thought
8　　maybe a new pair of shoes would help.
9　GINGER:　What brand have you been using?
10　BILL:　The New International Version.
11　GINGER:　Those shoes were made for walking, and that's just
12　　what they'll do. I don't know why you would be having
13　　trouble with them.
14　BILL:　Well, frankly, I've been experiencing a lack of support.
15　GINGER:　The problem may not be the shoe. How long have
16　　you been walking as a Christian?
17　BILL:　About five years.
18　GINGER:　Do you get together with other walkers?
19　BILL:　Every Sunday. I like to meet with everyone and talk
20　　and sing about walking. And I love to hear Coach Glossi

1   *(Name of your pastor)* **tell us all about how God wants us**
2   **to walk. I always leave all fired up and ready to walk**
3   **around the clock.** *(Sigh)* **But then on Monday morning . . .**
4   **GINGER: Mondays are tough?**
5   **BILL: The whole week is hard. That's when I feel**
6   **unsupported.**
7   **GINGER: Who do you usually walk with during the week?**
8   **BILL: No one.**
9   **GINGER:** *(Astonished)* **You walk alone?**
10   **BILL: Yup.**
11   **GINGER: Why?**
12   **BILL: How else can you do it?**
13   **GINGER: You know what I would do in your shoes?** *(BILL*
14   *shakes his head.)* **I'd join a walkers' group.**
15   **BILL:** *(Light bulb over the head, the sun dawning, realization*
16   *sweeping over him)* **Of course! I should join a walkers'**
17   **group. What's a walkers' group?**
18   **GINGER: It's a group that usually meets once a week for**
19   **support of other walkers. The group I am in has only six**
20   **other people. We tell each other how our Christian walk**
21   **is going. We hold each other accountable and learn how**
22   **to follow in God's footsteps. With that group and the large**
23   **walkers' group on Sunday, I stay in good shape.**
24   **BILL: I need to find a group like that. I don't like to walk**
25   **alone.**
26   **GINGER: You're welcome to come to our group. In fact, this**
27   **week we are going to go to a prison and talk about**
28   **walking. We call it a walk out.**
29   **BILL: Thanks. I just might do that. In any case, I don't think**
30   **I need a new pair of shoes. I think the old ones will do**
31   **me just fine.**
32   **GINGER: Hey, if the shoe fits, wear it.** *(Freeze)*
33
34
35

Shoot for the Stars

THEME: **Humbleness** — God uses the average, the weak, and the insignificant by human standards to accomplish his ends in our world.

SCRIPTURE: **I Corinthians 1:27** — "But God chose the foolish things of the world to shame the wise; God chose the weak things of the world to shame the strong."

SYNOPSIS: At a talent agency, the most average and humble person gets the best acting job.

CHARACTERS: Talent Agency Representative — All business (Male or Female).
Stella — Wants to be a glamorous movie star.
Billy Cruise — Confident, experienced.
Kevin Wright — Average kind of guy, new to acting, eager for any work.
Narrator

PROPS: Three envelopes with three pieces of note paper, folded up inside.

SETTING: A talent agency. Place two chairs side by side Center Stage.

"My name will be a household word."

1　*(Scene opens with STELLA and KEVIN seated. There should*
2　*be some space between their chairs. BILLY is standing behind*
3　*them and is in conversation with KEVIN who listens very*
4　*respectfully. STELLA should be rather nervous — chewing gum*
5　*perhaps.)*
6　**BILLY:　So take it from me, kid. You've got to sell yourself.**
7　**Be aggressive. Be proud. If you're going to be an actor,**
8　**you've got to bluff your way in. Never let them know your**
9　**shortcomings or insecurities.**
10　**STELLA:　Always, always act like you know what you're**
11　**doing.**
12　**BILLY:　And start at the top — don't take any dumb jobs.**
13　**REP:　*(Walks on and speaks almost monotone, very bored.)* "Shoot**
14　**for the Stars Talent Agency" has three jobs today.**
15　**Remember, please don't open your envelope until all the**
16　**jobs have been given out. The first** *(Reads off of the envelope)*
17　**is for a humble, average kind of person who knows he's**
18　**not a great actor but is willing to learn from one of the**
19　**best directors in the business!** *(STELLA and BILLY avoid*
20　*the agent's eyes. KEVIN stands up.)*

1   KEVIN: I'll take it. I'm willing to learn and be directed.

2   BILLY: *(To KEVIN in a stage whisper)* It's no good! Great
3   producers and directors don't want average people!

4   STELLA: *(Rolls her eyes.)* You'll be directed right out of the
5   business.

6   REP: The second job is for a woman who has the potential to
7   be the next Vanna White.

8   STELLA: *(Jumps up.)* That's for me! *(Takes envelope.)* My name
9   will be a household word.

10   REP: The third job is for someone who has the wit of Billy
11   Crystal and the looks of Tom Cruise.

12   BILLY: *(Clears his throat.)* That sounds like it has my name
13   on it.

14   REP: What *is* your name by the way?

15   BILLY: Billy Cruise.

16   REP: That's it for today. Good luck. *(They all open their
17   envelopes.)*

18   STELLA: Oh no! Not another dog food commercial.

19   BILLY: Oh rats! Another Sandu modeling job for J. C. Penney.

20   KEVIN: Sandu?!

21   BILLY: S and U — socks and underwear.

22   KEVIN: *(Excitedly)* Listen to this! I got a major motion picture!
23   "Legendary Hollywood director wants an average and
24   humble guy who is willing to be directed to play opposite
25   Julia Roberts in a new blockbuster film." It says, "we're
26   looking for someone who realizes that the story is most
27   important and the actors are merely players in the drama."

28   BILLY: Say . . . *(Puts his arm around KEVIN)* how about giving
29   this job to someone who is *really* humble? *(Freeze)*

30   NARRATOR: Just like the director wants an actor he could
31   mold and direct to fit the part, so God often calls those
32   who are not influential or wise by the world's standards
33   to people his drama of life. God's plan for the world does
34   not rely on people of wisdom, stature or power; he simply
35   needs people who are faithful.

The Show Home

THEME: **Obedience** — Building our lives on God gives us a strong foundation for life.

SCRIPTURE: **Matthew 7:24** — "Everyone who hears these words of mine and puts them into practice is like a wise man who built his house on the rock."

SYNOPSIS: A couple buying a house serves as a metaphor for building our lives wisely.

CHARACTERS: Lionel — Easygoing realtor
Becky and Curt — Home buyers

COSTUMES: Lionel should be dressed up.

PROPS: None.

SETTING: A show home. The "house" should be blocked out with masking tape or well rehearsed so that the inspection of the house is consistent with all three actors.

"This house has weathered many storms, but it still looks great."

1   *(Scene opens with LIONEL miming the opening of the front door*
2   *and showing the couple in. When the actors are not speaking,*
3   *they can be looking at different features of the house.)*
4   **LIONEL:** *(As he opens the front door)* **Now this house has been a**
5   **show home for many years and it always shows well. This**
6   **is a good example of a first rate house that you could**
7   **build, but only if you two are willing to pay the price.**
8   **BECKY:** **Ohhh,** *(Looking around)* **this is gorgeous.**
9   **CURT:** **No kidding. Lionel, this is one nice home.**
10   **LIONEL:** **Yes, this house was well built and has had the best**
11   **possible care. As a real estate agent, I can honestly say**
12   **that this is one of the best model homes I know of.**
13   **CURT:** **How old is this place?**
14   **LIONEL:** **I'd say about sixty-five years.**
15   **CURT:** **It sure doesn't look that old.** *(Walking forward to inspect*
16   *the walls)* **See, Becky, there are no cracks in the drywall.**
17   **LIONEL:** **That's because the builder put in a top notch**
18   **foundation; he built this house on Jesus Christ.**
19   **BECKY:** **You mean this house is built on solid rock?**
20   **LIONEL:** **That's right. But the builder didn't stop there. He**

1   used top quality materials in every step of the
2   construction.
3   BECKY: What do you mean, Lionel?
4   LIONEL: Well, when it comes to laying in the floor or putting
5   up the walls, some builders don't use materials that
6   support that first-time decision to build on Jesus Christ.
7   CURT: I've heard about houses like that. They have a great
8   foundation, but the walls are made of junk. Those houses
9   don't stand the test of time.
10   BECKY: You can just tell there is real strength in these walls.
11   Would that come from daily Bible reading?
12   LIONEL: Exactly. God's word is the best thing to use in the
13   construction of walls.
14   BECKY: *(Walking over to a window)* I'm also impressed by the
15   beautiful windows and the dignity of the archways. Some
16   thoughtful planning went into the design of this house.
17   LIONEL: That reflects time spent in prayer. A wise builder
18   works according to God's plan for the house. The plan is
19   revealed through God's word, but also in prayer.
20   CURT: I've heard that if a house is built right, it will mature
21   and become seasoned and increase in value.
22   LIONEL: That's true, Curt. This house has weathered many
23   storms, I'm sure, but it still looks great. That means the
24   builder made many little daily maintenance decisions
25   that supported that first-time decision to build a house.
26   CURT: In other words, following Jesus for a lifetime.
27   LIONEL: That's right. But many builders don't make the
28   right decisions. I end up showing many homes of inferior
29   construction built with conventional wisdom and pop
30   psychology.
31   BECKY: Yeah, I'll bet a lot of builders start with quality
32   materials and just get sidetracked or overwhelmed by
33   the cost.
34   CURT: And it would be easy to go for what's popular and
35   trendy instead of what's best. The best can be expensive.

1 LIONEL: *(Nodding his head)* **The cost of building a house like**
2 **this is high. It will take everything you have and are.**
3 CURT: **But look at what that cost can give you. This is one**
4 **exceptional home. I would say it's well worth the price.**
5 BECKY: **I agree.**
6 CURT: *(Down to business)* **OK, Lionel, if we want to build a**
7 **home like this, we need to build on Jesus Christ and daily**
8 **make   wise   building   decisions   that   reflect   our**
9 **commitment to God's plan for the house, like spending**
10 **time in Bible reading and prayer. Is that right?**
11 LIONEL: **That's what you would need to do. And, of course,**
12 **you would then furnish your house and keep it warm**
13 **and loving by worshiping weekly. What do you think?**
14 BECKY: *(Looks at her husband.)* **Well, I think this is exactly the**
15 **kind of house we would like to build.**
16 CURT: **I think so too. So, Lionel, what's the first thing we will**
17 **need to do to make Jesus Christ the foundation of our**
18 **house?** *(Freeze)*
19
20
21
22
23
24
25
26
27
28
29
30
31
32
33
34
35

Some Paint and Wallpaper

THEME: Change

SCRIPTURE: **Philippians 1:6** — "He who began a good work in you will carry it on to completion until the day of Christ Jesus."

SYNOPSIS: While redecorating a bedroom, two women learn how God changes us bit by bit, just as a room is transformed by paint and wallpaper.

CHARACTERS: Marcia — Mother of a five-year-old
Lori — A friend

COSTUMES: "Grubbies" for Marcia (paint-splattered jeans, an old shirt, etc.).

PROPS: Coffee cup, painting equipment (brushes, etc.) could be used but is not necessary. All painting could be mimed.

SETTING: A bedroom in the process of being redecorated. Place a stool or stepladder slightly off to one side.

1   *(Scene opens with MARCIA squinting and looking up at the top*
2   *of the imaginary [or fourth] wall. She should be facing the*
3   *congregation. She then bends down and dips her brush in the*
4   *paint and begins to work. MARCIA should hum or sing under*
5   *her breath as she works. LORI enters carrying a coffee cup.)*
6   **LORI:**   *(Looking around the room)* **Oh, Marcia, I love what you're**
7   **doing with the nursery.**
8   **MARCIA:**   **Hi, Lori. Well, actually this isn't the nursery**
9   **anymore. That's why I have to redecorate in here.**
10   **Brittany will be five in two weeks.**
11   **LORI:**   *(Motioning to an imaginary area on the wall)* **What**
12   **happened here?**
13   **MARCIA:**   *(Trying to put it positively)* **Brittany "expressed"**
14   **herself through the use of magic markers and crayons.**
15   **LORI:**   **Ohhh, she uses very colorful language.**
16   **MARCIA:**   *(Laughs.)* **Luckily she couldn't read or write yet.**
17   **LORI:**   *(Looks up the wall.)* **How did she get it all the way up**
18   **here?**
19   **MARCIA:**   **She broke up some of the crayons and threw them**
20   **at the wall.**
21   **LORI:**   *(Shakes her head.)* **What a creative kid. Do you need any**
22   **help?**
23   **MARCIA:**   **No, thanks, I'm almost done.** *(Steps back and looks at*
24   *her work.)* **When I am finished with this room, it will be**
25   **completely different.**
26   **LORI:**   *(Sitting down on a stool or a stepladder and sighing)* **I wish**
27   **it would only take some paint and wallpaper to make *me***
28   **completely different.**
29   **MARCIA:**   *(Continues painting.)* **What do you mean?**
30   **LORI:**   *(Takes a sip of coffee.)* **Sometimes it seems like it's taking**
31   **forever to become who God wants me to be.**
32   **MARCIA:**   **I've felt like that. Change can be painfully slow at**
33   **times.**
34   **LORI:**   **It would be so much easier if God just did a complete**
35   **makeover all at once, instead of working gradually from**

1   the inside out! I feel like I am stalled — that nothing is
2   really happening in me.
3   MARCIA: Often we are changing and we don't even notice it.
4   LORI: That's hard to believe.
5   MARCIA: Well, the Scripture says that "God began a good
6   work in us and that he will continue to do so until it is
7   finished." [1] I think God changes us bit by bit, making us
8   who he wants us to be.
9   LORI: I wish he would let me see more change, Marcia. When
10   I look at myself, all I can see is the stuff I don't like.
11   MARCIA: *(Stepping back and looking at the wall)* Lori, when you
12   look at this wall, what do you notice?
13   LORI: Hmmm ... a very dirty wall covered with chocolate
14   handprints and scribbling, with a little spot of clean,
15   fresh paint, of course.
16   MARCIA: But if I keep painting, then what will you see?
17   LORI: More and more of the paint and less of the old wall.
18   MARCIA: *(Stops painting.)* Lori, I am changing this room one
19   brush stroke at a time, and though it doesn't seem like
20   much, soon the room will be totally different. This is how
21   God works in our lives. He is like a master redecorator.
22   At first, all we can see is the old room, but he paints and
23   wallpapers, so to speak, and soon a new us begins to
24   emerge as a result of all his steady work.
25   LORI: The Master Redecorator. I like that. And you really do
26   think he works on us all the time?
27   MARCIA: I do.
28   LORI: *(Slyly)* You don't think he's taking a coffee break on
29   me right now?
30   MARCIA: I think *you* are taking a coffee break on you right now.
31   LORI: Yeah, you may be right about that ...
32   MARCIA: Well, if I'm going to finish this wall I need to move
33   the dresser. Lori, could you please give me a hand? *(LORI gets*
34   *up to help and they freeze when they bend down to move the dresser.)*
35   [1] *Paraphrase of Philippians 1:6*

The Ten Guidelines

THEME: **The Ten Commandments** — They are guidelines to help us live our lives the way God intended.

SCRIPTURE: **Exodus 20** — The Ten Commandments.

SYNOPSIS: A Toy Maker explains how his toys work better when they are used according to the directions he encloses.

CHARACTERS: Toy Maker
Customer
Doll 1 — Actual person
Doll 2 — Actual person

COSTUMES: Toy Maker may wear a bib apron. Dolls 1 and 2 may dress à la Raggedy Ann or Andy if they wish.

PROPS: None.

SETTING: The Toy Maker's shop where he builds and repairs toys (as in *Pinocchio*). Set a stool Center Stage for the Toy Maker to sit on as he/she works.

"You haven't been following the instructions, have you?"

1 *(Scene opens with the TOY MAKER working on DOLL 1. The*
2 *doll should look quite pleasant, relaxed and content.)*
3 **TOY MAKER: This is how I make my dolls: Sturdy, good-**
4 **looking and constructed from the highest quality**
5 **materials. Of course, this one is rather funny looking for**
6 **some reason . . . well, every doll *is* unique, but each comes**
7 **with the same instructions. Basically they all work the**
8 **same way.** *(TOY MAKER pats the head and DOLL 1 smiles.*
9 *He then pats her on the shoulder, and she turns her head toward*
10 *him. He pats her tummy and she burps.)* **Hmmm, this one still**
11 **needs a little work. Yeah, I include instructions with each**
12 **doll — The Ten Guidelines. They help to make sure that**
13 **each doll will last a long time and be happy. I invented**
14 **these dolls so I guess I should know what's best for them.**
15 *(Chuckles to himself. CUSTOMER bursts in pulling DOLL 2*
16 *behind him/her. DOLL 2 should look upset and angry.)*
17 **CUSTOMER: This dumb doll doesn't work anymore!**
18 **TOY MAKER: It doesn't? What has happened to it?**
19 **CUSTOMER: Look at it. Does it look right to you?**
20 **TOY MAKER: It certainly looks very unhappy!**

1 CUSTOMER: Watch this . . . *(CUSTOMER knocks it on the head*
2 *like knocking on a door, the toy frowns. He slaps it on the shoulder*
3 *and the head rolls back on its shoulders, mouth open and tongue*
4 *hanging out.)* **Listen to what it says when I hit it in the**
5 **stomach . . .**
6 TOY MAKER: *(Interrupting)* **No, please don't! You haven't**
7 **been following the instructions, have you?**
8 CUSTOMER: **What instructions?**
9 TOY MAKER: **Each of these dolls comes with a set of**
10 **instructions so the doll will last longer and be happier.**
11 CUSTOMER: **Oh, the Ten Guidelines that were in the box**
12 **when I got it? Nobody goes by those anymore.**
13 TOY MAKER: **Actually very many people do, but I gather**
14 **that you don't. Look at your doll. If you had followed the**
15 **instructions, this wouldn't have happened.**
16 CUSTOMER: **Listen, Toy Maker, cut the lecture. Can you fix**
17 **my doll? The kids are going crazy without it.**
18 TOY MAKER: **Of course I can fix it. I can make all things new,**
19 **but unless you follow the instructions this time, you'll be**
20 **back real soon with all the same problems.**
21 CUSTOMER: **Just fix the doll!** *(CUSTOMER exits.)*
22 TOY MAKER: **Let's see . . .** *(Looks at the nape of the neck of DOLL*
23 *2.)* **My goodness, you are only one year old! That's what**
24 **happens when your owner doesn't go by the instructions:**
25 **you wear out and age fast.** *(Shakes his head.)* **The**
26 **instructions are simple guidelines that make complete**
27 **sense. Honestly, I invented these dolls, so shouldn't I**
28 **know what's best for them?** *(Goes back to DOLL 1.)* **Now,**
29 **where was I? Oh yes, I was working on your vocals.** *(Makes*
30 *adjustment to the mouth of DOLL 1.)* **There. Let's try that!**
31 *(TOY MAKER pats the head and the doll smiles. He then pats*
32 *her on the shoulder and she turns her head toward him. He pats*
33 *the doll on the tummy, the doll opens her mouth and nothing*
34 *comes out. The TOY MAKER leans in to take a look, and the*
35 *doll promptly burps! Freeze)*

$325.00

THEME: **World Relief** — We have a responsibility for those less fortunate than we are, including both those of the household of faith and the world in general.

SCRIPTURE: **Matthew 25:45** — " 'Whatever you did not do for one of the least of these, you did not do for me.' "

SYNOPSIS: A man who has just spent $325.00 on a rare book dreams that he is eating in a restaurant and a starving child comes up and looks in the window at him. The book buyer realizes that he should help everyone — not just those to whom he has emotional or relational ties.

CHARACTERS: Dean
Robin
(husband and wife)

COSTUMES: Two bathrobes.

PROPS: Book, brochure.

SETTING: The living room in the middle of the night. Place two chairs side by side Center Stage for a sofa.

"Robin, I had a bad dream."

1   *(Scene opens with DEAN pacing back and forth with an old book*
2   *and a brochure in his hands.)*
3   **DEAN:**   *(Distraught)* **Three hundred and twenty-five dollars . . .**
4   **three hundred and twenty-five dollars . . . I can't believe**
5   **I spent that much on a book.** *(ROBIN enters, very sleepy.)*
6   **ROBIN:**   **Dean, it's the middle of the night. What are you doing**
7   **up?**
8   **DEAN:**   **Robin, I paid three hundred and twenty-five dollars**
9   **for this book today at the auction.**
10   **ROBIN:**   *(Yawns)* **I know, you told me. You said it was a great**
11   **deal.**
12   **DEAN:**   **You don't understand! I paid three hundred and**
13   **twenty-five dollars for a** *book!*
14   **ROBIN:**   **You've paid more for other books, Dean. That's your**
15   **hobby, remember? I collect shoes, you collect rare books.**
16   *(Looks at her watch.)* **Oh my goodness, it's three twenty-five**
17   **in the morning! Come back to bed before you wake the**
18   **boys.**
19   **DEAN:**   **I can't.**
20   **ROBIN:**   **Why not?**

1   DEAN: I had a bad dream.

2   ROBIN: *This* is a bad dream. If I don't get my beauty sleep,

3   no one will recognize me in the morning! *(Yawns.)* I think

4   I'm having to sleep longer and longer these days just to

5   maintain my beauty . . .

6   DEAN: Robin, I had a dream; it troubles me.

7   ROBIN: *(Still sleepy)* This isn't the same one where you

8   dreamt you ate the huge marshmallow and when you

9   woke up the pillow was gone?!

10   DEAN: *(Indignant)* I don't remember that!

11   ROBIN: You burped feathers for three days. Come on, Dean,

12   let's go back to bed.

13   DEAN: *(Sitting)* Robin, come here and sit beside me. *(ROBIN*

14   *sits.)* I dreamt I was on a business trip in some third world

15   country. I was sitting in a restaurant by a window and

16   eating when a group of children came by and looked in

17   at me.

18   ROBIN: Staring children always terrify me too! Once when

19   I was at Sears . . .

20   DEAN: These children were starving.

21   ROBIN: Well, the kids at Sears looked pretty hungry too!

22   DEAN: No, I mean these children were really starving. They

23   looked in at the mounds of hot steaming food on my table.

24   Hunger was etched on their weary faces. But I looked at

25   them and told them to leave. I said, "This is my food and

26   I have worked hard for it."

27   ROBIN: If you worked hard then you must have had a

28   different job in your dream than you do in real life . . .

29   DEAN: They just kept staring at the food and devouring it

30   with their eyes so I reached over and began to shut the

31   blinds . . .

32   ROBIN: *(Aghast)* Dean, you shouldn't have done that. You

33   should always ask the waitress to shut them for you.

34   DEAN: But as the blinds were closing, their faces changed

35   and they became our boys. I grabbed the food and ran

1   outside to give it to Derek and Aaron, but they were gone.

2   And as I looked for them I kept thinking, "I pray to God

3   that someone will find them and give them something to

4   eat."

5   ROBIN: *(Completely awake now)* **Our boys were hungry?**

6   DEAN: Yes.

7   ROBIN: But God wouldn't let our boys go hungry. He loves

8   them.

9   DEAN: I think God loves all children and I don't think he

10   lets anyone go hungry. I think *we* do ...

11   ROBIN: I wish you had dreamt about the marshmallow

12   again ...

13   DEAN: When I woke up, I kept hearing those lines from the

14   Bible when the people being judged asked God, "Lord,

15   when did we see you hungry or thirsty or a stranger or

16   needing clothes or sick or in prison, and did not help

17   you?" And the Lord replied, "Whatever you did not do

18   for the least of these, you did not do for me." [1]

19   ROBIN: *(Shivers)* **I'm glad it was only a dream. It probably**

20   means nothing.

21   DEAN: *(Staring at her)* **After that dream I couldn't sleep, so I**

22   came down here to get something to drink, all the while

23   thinking we are responsible for people we don't even

24   know. As I passed the coffee table, I noticed a pamphlet

25   from one of those mission agencies ...

26   ROBIN: Yeah, it just came today. We get those all the time.

27   DEAN: Well, across the top of this brochure it said, "Support

28   a family of four for a year in a Third World country."

29   ROBIN: Did it say how much?

30   DEAN: It did ... it said three hundred twenty-five dollars.

31   *(Freeze)*

32

33

34

35   *[1] Paraphrase of Matthew 25:44, 45*

Time, Talent, Treasure

THEME: Giving — When we give our "all" to Jesus, it includes our material resources.

SCRIPTURE: Three biblical examples of possessions used to glorify Jesus:
Matthew 21:1-7, Mark 11:1-6, Luke 19:28-25
A donkey
John 6:1-13
5 loaves and 2 fishes
Luke 7:36-38
Expensive perfume

SYNOPSIS: On the talk show *Time, Talent, Treasure,* three Bible characters relate how they gave of their material resources to further the work of the kingdom of God. The point is made that we never know how what we possess may be of value to God.

CHARACTERS: Shawn Smiler — Talk show host
Matthias — Donkey owner
Joshua — The boy with the loaves and fishes
Sarah — Woman who pours perfume on Jesus' feet

COSTUMES: Either biblical robes or contemporary dress will work.

PROPS: Microphone.

SETTING: The set of a game show. Set a podium Center Stage for Shawn.

1   *(Scene opens with SHAWN SMILER running On-stage like game*
2   *show hosts often do. The other three characters are spread*
3   *throughout the congregation. They stand as SHAWN calls on*
4   *them.)*
5   **SHAWN:**   Hello, hello, hello, and welcome to my new show,
6   *Time, Talent, Treasure.* This is the totally new,
7   innovative, cutting edge, going out on a limb, throwing
8   caution to the wind, unique to our network, show where
9   we find out how you, the studio audience, are using your
10   time, talent or treasure to further the work of God. Today
11   we want to hear how you have used your *treasure* for the
12   cause of Christ. So what are we waiting for? Let's get
13   started! I have a list here of all of you in our studio
14   audience today, so I'll just call a name at
15   random . . . Ah . . . Matthias Barburro. *(All hyped up)* **Tell**
16   **us how you have used your treasure for the cause of**
17   **Christ!**
18   **MATTHIAS:**   *(Stands.)* Well, I am a poor man. I never have any
19   extra money. We just have enough to take care of our
20   basic needs. I remember when I first heard about Jesus.
21   Now, he was a poor man too, but he was taking time off
22   from his trade to preach and heal. The wife and I wanted
23   to help Jesus, but since we had no money, there was
24   nothing we could do but pray for the success of his work.
25   Then one day about two years later, a couple of
26   Jesus' disciples showed up at my door asking to use my
27   donkey! It really was all that I had to give. I hadn't had
28   the donkey very long, but I wanted to help, so I gave it
29   to them. As they left, I wondered whether or not two
30   fishermen would know what to do with a donkey! But
31   then, later, I saw Jesus ride that donkey of mine into
32   Jerusalem while the people cheered and shouted and
33   waved palm branches. I was pretty proud. Who would
34   have thought that Jesus could use a donkey? Who would
35   have thought that the one thing I had to give, Jesus

1   **needed.** *(MATTHIAS sits.)*

2   **SHAWN:**   Thank you very much, Mr. Barburro. I would have

3   never thought of a donkey as a treasure, but . . . let's

4   see . . . another person . . . *(Looks down his list.)* **Sarah of**

5   **Jericho.** Where are you, Sarah? Ah, there you are. Tell

6   us how you have used *your* treasure for the cause of

7   Christ!

8   **SARAH:**   *(Stands.)* My name is Sarah of Jericho. I have lived a

9   less than honorable life, and many people will not

10   associate with me as a result. But Jesus was not afraid

11   to be seen with me. I felt such love from him — like he

12   looked past my sin to who I really was inside.

13   Anyway, one night an important Pharisee held a

14   dinner party and invited Jesus. He treated Jesus poorly,

15   however, and didn't even have his servants wash Jesus'

16   feet. I was in the crowd of onlookers lining the court. I

17   had brought a jar of perfume to give to Jesus to support

18   his work. He and his disciples lived on donations, you

19   know. But when I saw how Simon treated Jesus, the man

20   who loved everyone, I began to cry. I pushed through the

21   people to where Jesus was seated and knelt at his feet

22   and washed them with my hair and tears. Then I poured

23   the perfume on his feet. It ran all down his toes, over the

24   tiles, through the cracks and into the earth. The

25   Pharisees criticized me, for the perfume was worth a

26   year's wages, but love is not always practical. Sometimes

27   a gift has no practical purpose besides that of expressing

28   love, and I loved Jesus. *(SARAH sits.)*

29   **SHAWN:**   Amazing. Thank you, Sarah. Who would have

30   thought both a donkey and perfume could be used by

31   God? We have time for one more story . . . Joshua Bar

32   Wonder. Tell us how you have used *your* treasure for the

33   cause of Christ!

34   **JOSHUA:**   *(Stands.)* My name is Joshua Bar Wonder, the son of

35   Wonder. My dad is a baker. You may know him — he's

1 famous for his Wonder bagels. One day Jesus came to a
2 hill near our town to speak. I remember the posters with
3 the catchy title "Jesus — Live in Concert: Coming to a
4 Hill Near You." I really wanted to hear him, so my dad
5 packed me a lunch of five small Wonder barley loaves
6 and two tiny fishes. Usually Jesus spoke all day, so I
7 figured if I had a lunch, I could stay as long as he talked.
8 Towards late afternoon, the crowd, about five thousand
9 people, grew restless. They were hungry. It turned out I
10 was the only person who had any food with me. Jesus
11 had all the people sit down and then he took my lunch,
12 the five small loaves of Wonder barley bread and the two
13 tiny fishes. He said a blessing, and then his disciples
14 began to pass the lunch around. Five thousand people
15 kept taking and taking and there was still more and more.
16 By the end, there were twelve baskets of Wonder barley
17 bread left over. It was incredible! I said it was a miracle,
18 and my dad said it was good advertising! But I'm *still*
19 amazed that as little as I had, when I gave it to Jesus, he
20 made so much more out of it. *(JOSHUA sits.)*
21 SHAWN: Thank you, Joshua Bar Wonder. There you have
22 it — what these people had to give, God used: a donkey,
23 perfume and a sack lunch. What do *you* have that God
24 wants to use? Well, we're out of time. Thank you for
25 joining us for *Time, Talent, and Treasure.* Tune in next
26 week for three more true live stories from you about how
27 you've used your time, talent or treasure.
28
29
30
31
32
33
34
35

The Weight Lifter

THEME: **Hypocrisy** — If we really believe in Jesus Christ, then our actions will not belie that fact.

SCRIPTURE: **Titus 1:16** — "They claim to know God, but by their actions they deny him."

SYNOPSIS: At a weightlifting competition, a person who has talked his way in finds that it takes more than talk to compete. As Christians, it is not enough to talk of our knowledge of God — our actions must bear out our beliefs.

CHARACTERS: TV interviewer
Sam — Weight lifter (a smaller kid or skinny adult, someone who obviously doesn't lift weights)

COSTUMES: Suit and tie for the interviewer, athletic attire for the weight lifter.

PROPS: Microphone.

SETTING: A televised weightlifting competition.

1   *(Scene opens with the rapid-fire commentary of the TV*
2   *ANNOUNCER.)*
3   **TV ANNOUNCER: Hey, we're back after that brief**
4   **commercial message. We are broadcasting live from the**
5   **wide, wonderful, wacky world of weightlifting. Here**
6   **comes our next competitor.** *(WEIGHT LIFTER comes onto*
7   *the stage flexing his muscles. He should look pretty phony.)* **And**
8   **here he is, Sliding Slight Sam. How are you doing, Slight**
9   **Sam?**
10   **SAM:** *(Gruffly, trying to be macho)* **Oh, I'm doing pretty good,**
11   **pretty good.**
12   **TV ANNOUNCER: If you don't mind me saying, you look a**
13   **little small to be a weight lifter.**
14   **SAM: Well, looks aren't everything.**
15   **TV ANNOUNCER: No, I guess you're right. What kind of**
16   **training have you done?**
17   **SAM: I've trained with the best. I even trained with Hulk**
18   **Hogan for awhile.**
19   **TV ANNOUNCER: Hulk Hogan? Why would you train with**
20   **him? He's a wrestler!**
21   **SAM: Oh, right. It must have been his brother, Paul Hogan.**
22   **TV ANNOUNCER: What other kind of training have you had,**
23   **Slight Sam? I just find it hard to believe that with your**
24   **build, you are actually a weight lifter.**
25   **SAM:** *(Flexing all the while he talks)* **Well, I trained with an**
26   **Olympic team.**
27   **TV ANNOUNCER:** *(Astonished)* **You trained with the Olympic**
28   **Weightlifting Team?**
29   **SAM: Well, not quite . . .**
30   **TV ANNOUNCER: Well, either you did or you didn't. Did you**
31   **train with the Olympic Weightlifting Team?**
32   **SAM: Well . . . actually, I swam in an olympic-sized pool once.**
33   **TV ANNOUNCER:** *(Very sketpical)* **Hmmm . . . well, it looks**
34   **like the judges are ready. We will see if Sliding Slight**
35   **Sam can actually lift as well as he can talk.** *(SAM mimes*

1   *putting his hands on the bar and proceeds to try and lift it, but*

2   *obviously he cannot.)*

3   **TV ANNOUNCER:** *(Narrating as SAM attempt to lift)* **His hands**

4   **are on the bar. He's starting to lift. He's trying ... he's**

5   **trying ... he's still trying ... and ...** *(As SAM gives up)* **he**

6   **cannot do it. All talk and no lift, I'd say. Sam, what**

7   **happened? You seemed so confident. You said you could**

8   **do it. It was only one hundred pounds!**

9   **SAM:** **I don't know what happened! Just this morning I lifted**

10   **two hundred and fifty pounds.**

11   **TV ANNOUNCER:** **Sure, Sam, sure. Well, that's about it from**

12   **here and the wide, wonderful, wacky, and I might add**

13   **weird world of weightlifting. As for Sam, he claimed to**

14   **know weightlifting, but his actions denied it. My dog**

15   **could've done better than that! That's all for now. Please**

16   **stay tuned for our next competition: live tuna fish**

17   **wrestling each other in vats of Jello pudding.**

18

19

20

21

22

23

24

25

26

27

28

29

30

31

32

33

34

35

What Goes Around

THEME: **Parental respect** — The fifth commandment.

SCRIPTURE: **Exodus 20:12** — "Honor your father and your mother . . ."

SYNOPSIS: A woman is quite concerned because her son seems to have lost respect for her and she cannot understand why. In the second scene she visits her mother and we find that she has no respect for her mother either.

CHARACTERS: Peggy, A typical 90s mom
Jay — Peggy's slightly out of control junior high son
June — Peggy's mom, an older lady living in a rest home

COSTUMES: June should dress for her years — perhaps a shawl over a print dress.

PROPS: A bowl of apples, knitting or crochet work, mixing bowl and spoon.

SETTING: Scene I is set in Peggy's kitchen. On one side of the stage, set up a small table to hold the bowl of apples and the mixing bowl and spoon. Scene II takes place in a nursing home. On the other side of the stage, set up the same table with apples (minus mixing bowl), a rocking chair, and a folding chair.

1 **SCENE I**

2

3 *(Scene opens with PEGGY standing at the table mixing*

4 *something in a bowl. JAY enters.)*

5 **JAY:** *(As he crosses over to get an apple)* **Hi, Mom.**

6 **PEGGY:** *(Edge to her voice)* **Hey, I told you those apples were**

7 **for after dinner.**

8 **JAY:** **So?** *(He twists the stem off the apple.)*

9 **PEGGY:** **So don't take one.** *(Notices what he is doing with the*

10 *apple.)* **Where did you learn to twist off the stem of the**

11 **apple like that?**

12 **JAY:** **From you.**

13 **PEGGY:** **From me? No, I don't do that. You must have learned**

14 **that from your father.** *(JAY takes a bite.)* **Listen, I told you**

15 **not to eat that apple!** *(Grabs it from him.)* **You just don't**

16 **mind anymore.**

17 **JAY:** **Aw, Mom, don't start that again . . .**

18 **PEGGY:** **Jay, I'm still your mother, you listen to me.**

19 **JAY:** *(Big sigh of disgust)* **I'm listening . . .**

20 **PEGGY:** **Hey, you be respectful when I talk to you.**

21 **JAY:** *(Sarcastic)* **I'll bow next time I come into the room.**

22 **PEGGY:** **That's it! You're not so big that I still can't put you**

23 **over my knee.** *(Grabs him by the arm, and he pulls away.)*

24 **JAY:** *(Coldly)* **Be real, Mom, why should I respect you?** *(He*

25 *walks Off-stage.)*

26 **PEGGY:** *(Calls after him.)* **Who taught you to treat your**

27 **mother like that?** *(She exits. Stagehand quickly sets up the*

28 *second scene.)*

29

30 **SCENE II**

31

32 *(Scene opens with PEGGY's mother JUNE sitting in a rocking*

33 *chair, knitting or doing some kind of hand work. PEGGY is*

34 *sitting and as the scene starts, she gets up, takes an apple and*

35 *begins to twist the stem on it. She is clearly agitated.)*

1   JUNE: I just said it was nice to see you, that's all.
2   PEGGY: I heard you, Mother, but I know you. You're trying
3   to say I don't see you enough.
4   JUNE: Well, that goes without saying! I hardly ever see you
5   or the kids.
6   PEGGY: You don't know what it's like to raise a family today.
7   We're busy all the time . . .
8   JUNE: I raised four kids, and you stayed home the longest,
9   I recall.
10 PEGGY: . . . and any spare time we have, we want to spend
11   with the family.
12 JUNE: For heaven's sake, Peggy, I am your mother! Doesn't
13   that count as family anymore?
14 PEGGY: That's not what I meant.
15 JUNE: For twenty-four years I did your laundry. I fed and
16   clothed you. I held you. I . . .
17 PEGGY: *(Coldly)* I know. I know . . . I do those things now too.
18   What's the point?
19 JUNE: *(Softly)* I'm your mother, Peggy. It just seems like I at
20   least deserve some respect . . .
21 PEGGY: *(Briskly)* So it's the "I'm old and nobody cares about
22   me anymore" routine. Well, I have my frustrations as a
23   mother, too.
24 JUNE: Peggy . . .
25 PEGGY: *(Gathering up her things)* I need to go, Mother. Jason
26   has basketball the next three Sundays so it may be a few
27   weeks before I get back here.
28 JUNE: Thank you for coming . . . *(As PEGGY leaves)* Call me if
29   you can . . . *(Calling after her)* Peggy, I love you . . . *(Freeze)*
30
31
32
33
34
35

What on Earth Do You Do?

THEME: **Love** — The church is a caring body of people.

SCRIPTURE: **Mark 12:31** — "Love your neighbor as yourself."

SYNOPSIS: In the game show "What on Earth Do You Do?" panelists compete to find out what the guest does. It turns out he is simply a believer who loves his neighbor.

CHARACTERS: Shawn or Shawna Smiler — Talk show host
The Guest — Male or female
Three Panelists

COSTUMES: The talk show host should be dressed up.

PROPS: Microphone.

SOUND EFFECTS: Cassette of theme show-type music (optional).

SETTING: A TV game show set.

"Hey, hey, hey! Am I glad to see you! I'm Shawn Smiler!"

1   *(Scene opens with the three PANELISTS milling around making*
2   *small talk. Theme song type music should be playing. SHAWN*
3   *SMILER runs in.)*
4   **SHAWN: Hey, hey, hey! Am I glad to see you! Because I'm**
5   **Shawn Smiler, and it's time to play.**
6   **ALL:** *(Together with SHAWN)* **What on earth do you do?**
7   *(PANELISTS line up in order on SHAWN's right.)*
8   **SHAWN: Welcome, panelists.** *(GUEST enters and stands to*
9   *SHAWN's left.)* **Our mystery guest today works with**
10 **people. Remember the rules: You each get three**
11 **questions but only one guess. Let's start with you,**
12 **_____.** *(Name of PANELIST 1)*
13 **PANELIST 1: OK, mystery guest, do you work with *lots* of**
14 **people?**
15 **GUEST: Yes.**
16 **PANELIST 2: Do you work with these people to help them**
17 **better themselves?**
18 **GUEST: Yes.**
19 **PANELIST 3: In your line of work, are you often encouraging**
20 **people?**

1   GUEST: Yes.

2   PANELIST: 3:   I think I know what our mystery guest does,

3   Shawn.

4   SHAWN: Go ahead, _____. *(Name of PANELIST 3)*

5   PANELIST 3: Well, he said he works with lots of people to

6   help them better themselves and that he often

7   encourages them. I think it's obvious that he is a pro

8   baseball coach. *(The other two contestants look at each other*

9   *like of course PANELIST 3 is right.)*

10   SHAWN: *(Big encouraging smile)* I'm afraid you are absolutely

11   wrong. But if the other two can't guess, you'll get another

12   chance. Let's continue the questions with _____

13   *(PANELIST 1)* again.

14   PANELIST 1: Thank you, Shawn. Mystery guest, can people

15   come to you for help?

16   GUEST: Yes.

17   PANELIST 3: Does your situation make you accepting of

18   their faults and shortcomings?

19   GUEST: Yes.

20   PANELIST 2: Do people come to you for help because they

21   can make friends and be accepted for who they are?

22   GUEST: Yes.

23   PANELIST 2: *(Triumphantly)* I know what he does for a living,

24   Shawn.

25   SHAWN: Give us your best guess, _____. *(PANELIST 2)*

26   PANELIST 2: He said that people can come to him for help,

27   and that where he works, they can find friends and be

28   accepted for who they are. He is . . . *(Pause for effect)* a

29   bartender.

30   SHAWN: Well, that's a good guess, but I'm afraid you're

31   wrong, too. Time is running out and so are the dollars.

32   One more round of questions. We go to you, _____.

33   *(Name of PANELIST 3)*

34   PANELIST 3: Do you get paid for your job?

35   GUEST: No. *(All PANELISTS gasp.)*

1   PANELIST 2:   Hmmm. So what you do is not so much your
2   means of living as much as it is your way of life?
3   GUEST: Yes.
4   PANELIST 1:   So your life is to care for others?
5   GUEST: Yes.
6   SHAWN: Time to take your guess, _____. *(Name of*
7   *PANELIST 1)*
8   PANELIST 1:   Boy, I don't know. I guess a volunteer of some
9   type because he doesn't get paid for what he does, but
10   he cares for people and has committed his whole life to
11   that.
12   SHAWN: Well, you are partly right, _____. *(PANELIST*
13   *1)* But that's not the whole story. Mystery guest, tell us
14   what you do and why.
15   GUEST: Actually I haven't committed my life to the service
16   of others as much as I have committed myself to Jesus
17   Christ. In being committed to him, I become concerned
18   for all people. In the book of Titus it says, "We must devote
19   ourselves to doing good so that we do not lead
20   unproductive lives."
21   PANELIST 2:   So What on Earth Do You Do?
22   GUEST: I am a follower of Jesus Christ.
23   ALL: *(Ad-lib)* Of course, I knew that all along. Oh, that was
24   easy. *(Etc.)*
25   SHAWN: That's the show for today, folks. Mystery guest, you
26   sure stumped the panel. Panelists, we probably won't
27   invite you back. *(Looks at the congregation.)* Tune in next
28   week when again we ask,
29   ALL: *(In unison)* **What on Earth Do You Do?**
30
31
32
33
34
35   *¹ Paraphrase of Titus 3:14*

Whose Party?

THEME: **Christmas** — Christmas is not just *any* celebration, but a celebration of Jesus' birth.

SCRIPTURE: **Luke 2** — The story of Jesus' birth.

SYNOPSIS: In this take-off of the *Twilight Zone,* "Rob Surly" introduces us to a room full of partiers. They are celebrating a birthday, but they can't remember whose birthday it is.

CHARACTERS: Rob Surly
9 Party goers (This sketch works great with kids about seven or eight years of age.)
Party goer extras, if desired

COSTUMES: Party goers should be dressed up in their best party clothes.

PROPS: Pop, snacks, birthday cake.

SETTING: A party. Set up a few small tables and chairs and put up a few balloons and other party decorations.

"That's it! That's it! A birthday party has to be for someone."

1   *(Scene opens with everybody on stage except for PARTY GOER*
2   *3. Everybody is frozen until ROB SURLY stops speaking.)*
3   **ROB SURLY: Imagine yourself in another dimension, a**
4   **dimension of space, a dimension of sound, a dimension**
5   **of *spirit*. Before you know it, you'll find yourself in ... the**
6   **Spirit zone. These people are trapped in an awful cycle**
7   **of yearly superficial birthday parties. These are just**
8   **ordinary people in an ordinary house caught in an**
9   **ordinary but embarrassing situation. But they are about**
10   **to find truth.**
11   **PARTY GOER 1:   Hey, great party!**
12   **PARTY GOER 2:   I know it! You come here every year?**
13   **PARTY GOER 1:   I wouldn't miss it!**
14   **PARTY GOER 3:   *(Coming from Off-stage with more pop)* Hey,**
15   **happy birthday everyone.**
16   **ALL: *(Ad-lib)* Yeah, happy birthday. What a great party. *(Etc.)***
17   **PARTY GOER 3:   Thanks for coming. I'm glad you reminded**
18   **me it was my turn to host the party. There's lots of pop**
19   **and chips. Later we'll have pizza. But for right now, party**
20   **hardy! Happy birthday! (*PARTY GOER 3 exits. PARTY***

1   *GOERS cheer and whoop it up. The party should continue in*

2   *the background while PARTY GOERS 4 and 5 have their*

3   *conversation.)*

4   **PARTY GOER 4:**   *(To PARTY GOER 5)* **You know, something's**

5   **not right here.**

6   **PARTY GOER 5:**   **What do you mean?**

7   **PARTY GOER 4:**   **I dunno. I can't put my finger on it.**

8   **PARTY GOER 5:**   **Aren't you having a good time?**

9   **PARTY GOER 4:**   **Sure I am, but is that the point . . . for *me* to**

10   **have a good time?**

11   **PARTY GOER 5:**   **Of course it is. It's a birthday party.**

12   **PARTY GOER 6:**   **Hey, everybody, I propose a toast to the best**

13   **birthday party ever!**

14   **ALL:**   **To the best birthday party ever!** *(Ad-lib)* **Happy**

15   **birthday, great party.** *(Etc.)*

16   **PARTY GOER 4:**   *(To PARTY GOER 5 again)* **I tell you,**

17   **something isn't right. I mean, why is this a birthday**

18   **party? Why not just an everyday party?**

19   **PARTY GOER 5:**   **Well . . . we have balloons.**

20   **PARTY GOER 4:**   **But that doesn't make it a birthday party.**

21   *(To the group)* **Hey everybody, listen. I don't want to put**

22   **a damper on things, but exactly why do we have a**

23   **birthday party every year? You know? Why not just a**

24   **regular party?**

25   **PARTY GOER 7:**   **It's a birthday party because we have a**

26   **birthday cake.**

27   **PARTY GOER 1:**   **Yeah, he's right.**

28   **PARTY GOER 8:**   **You don't have to know why you're having a**

29   **party. You just have one.**

30   **PARTY GOER 1:**   **Yeah, *she's* right.**

31   **PARTY GOER 9:**   **Don't try and analyze everything! We have**

32   **pop, chips, friends and games. It's a birthday party. What**

33   **more reason do you need?**

34   **PARTY GOER 4:**   **I like to party as much as the next guy, but**

35   **there has to be a reason for a birthday party. It seems to**

1 me there needs to be a reason beyond just getting
2 together to party.
3 PARTY GOER 1:   Yeah, *he's* right too.
4 PARTY GOER 2:   Hey, party-pooper, be quiet!
5 ALL: Yeah, pipe down or go home!
6 PARTY GOER 3:   *(Comes on with a birthday cake, singing)* **Happy**
7 **birthday to you,**
8 ALL: *(Joining in)* **Happy birthday to you. Happy birthday**
9 **dear . . . dear . . .** *(They trail off and look blankly at each other.)*
10 PARTY GOER 1:   Dear who?
11 PARTY GOER 4:   That's it! That's it! A birthday party has to
12 *be* for someone. Someone has to have a birthday.
13 PARTY GOER 2:   Nah, that can't be right.
14 PARTY GOER 4:   Sure, you have a birthday party to honor
15 someone who is having a birthday!
16 PARTY GOER 7:   *(Realization dawning)* So the focus of the
17 birthday party shouldn't be the party, but the *person*
18 whose birthday we are celebrating?
19 PARTY GOER 4:   I suppose.
20 PARTY GOER 8:   Should the guest of honor wear his birthday
21 suit so everybody will know it's his birthday?
22 ALL: *(Ad-lib)* Not! No way. Get outta here. *(Etc.)*
23 PARTY GOER 7:   So whose birthday *are* we celebrating?
24 *(They all look at each other and shrug their shoulders. Freeze)*
25 ROB SURLY: These people realize a significant point: A
26 birthday party should focus on *someone,* not on the
27 celebration. All over our world at this time of year, we
28 celebrate a birthday: Jesus' birth. It doesn't go without
29 saying, "Don't forget the reason for the season."
30
31
32
33
34
35

Wilson and Tilson
(When Worlds Collide)

THEME: **Priorities** — You cannot serve God and the world.

SCRIPTURE: **Matthew 6:24** — "No one can serve two masters. Either he will hate the one and love the other, or he will be devoted to the one and despise the other!"

SYNOPSIS: A woman who has two bosses finds that it is impossible to adequately serve them both equally. This highlights the dilemma we face if we try to juggle our service of God with that of the world.

CHARACTERS: Mr. Tilson — Large man
Mr. Wilson — Small man
Ms. Nilsson — Receptionist/administrative assistant

COSTUMES: Work attire.

PROPS: Three telephones if desired, or they may be mimed.

SETTING: Three separate offices in the same office building. Set up three chairs Center Stage.

1   *(Scene opens with MR. TILSON set up to the left of MS.*
2   *NILSSON and MR. WILSON set up to the right. MS. NILSSON*
3   *is working at a switchboard. When the people are on the phone*
4   *they should mime talking and listening.)*
5   **MRS. NILSSON:** *(With phone to her ear)* **Wilson and Tilson, Ms.**
6   **Nilsson speaking. Can I help you? Yes he is, hold**
7   **please** ... *(MR. WILSON picks up the phone.)* **Mr. Wilson?**
8   **Mr. Olson is on line one ... Wilson and Tilson, Ms. Nilsson**
9   **speaking. Can I help you? ... Yes he is, hold please ...**
10   *(MR. TILSON picks up his phone.)* **Mr. Tilson, Mr. Johnson**
11   **on line two ...**
12   **MR. WILSON:** **Not a problem, Mr. Olson. I'll have Ms. Nilsson**
13   **send a letter to Mr. Johnson on our behalf ...**
14   **MR. TILSON:** **I am happy to represent you in this matter.**
15   **Rest assured that I will have my assistant send a notice**
16   **to Mr. Olson and his lawyer right away.**
17   **MS. NILSSON:** **Wilson and Tilson, Ms. Nilsson speaking. Can**
18   **I help you? Mom? How's it going? ... Oh, I'm fine.**
19   **MR. TILSON:** **I can understand your need for complete**
20   **confidentiality in this matter. I will also make sure that**
21   **no one knows anything about this ... But Mr. Johnson,**
22   **are you positive that Mr. Olson is the guilty party?**
23   **MR. WILSON:** **The only way that this can work is if we can**
24   **maintain complete silence on the matter. Of course our**
25   **whole defense, Mr. Olson, will be based upon the**
26   **videotapes taken over four days that you accidentally**
27   **shot of Mr. Johnson. No one else must know ...**
28   **MS. NILSSON:** **No, Mom. I work equal time for both of them.**
29   **So far, it's been pretty easy to work for two bosses. Mr.**
30   **Wilson and Mr. Tilson are both nice men. I don't see how**
31   **there could be any kind of conflict ...**
32   **MR. WILSON:** **No, at this point I have no idea who Mr.**
33   **Johnson's lawyer could be. But it will be very important**
34   **that he not know who I am ...**
35   **MR. TILSON:** **The quicker we can get the letter to Mr. Olson's**

1 lawyer, the better off we will be. In fact, we will need to
2 get the notice sent before we close today or we may not
3 have a case when we get to court.
4 MS. NILSSON: Love you too, Mom. I'll call if anything
5 interesting happens.
6 MR. WILSON: Hmmm ... I didn't realize that ... That means
7 that we need to get a letter sent out to that effect by the
8 end of the day. My goodness, we have fifteen minutes
9 before the last mail pickup. Mr. Olson, I'll get right on it.
10 MR. TILSON: Listen, Mr. Johnson, I have to get this letter
11 done in the next fourteen minutes. That's the last mail
12 pickup for the day. Let me take care of it and call you
13 back. *(WILSON and TILSON both hang up their phones at the*
14 *same time and mime pushing intercom buttons on their phones.)*
15 WILSON and TILSON: Ms. Nilsson, could you please come in
16 here immediately to take a letter ... *(She looks up aghast with*
17 *the phone in her hand. Freeze)*
18 NARRATOR: Scripture tells us that we cannot serve two
19 masters. It is impossible to follow God and serve anything
20 or anyone else as well. If we try, those worlds will
21 eventually collide. We must choose one or the other.
22
23
24
25
26
27
28
29
30
31
32
33
34
35

SCRIPTURE INDEX

Sketches are arranged in alphabetical order throughout the book for easy reference.

TOPICAL INDEX

Each script is entered under three different headings for cross-reference purposes.
Sketches are arranged in alphabetical order throughout the book for easy reference.

186

School	*Grading on the Curve*
Second Coming	*Forever Life Insurance*
	The Phone Call
Sermon on the Mount	*Back to Back With Benny*
	Live! With Brock Tully
Serving	*Service*
Shaped by God	*The Bonsai Tree*
Spiritual Gifts	*Service*
	Time, Talent, Treasure
Spiritual Health	*The Health Club*
Spiritual Knowledge	*The Salesclerk*
	Sewing 101
Spiritual Maturity	*A Matter of Height*
Stewardship	*Let's Make a Tithe Deal*
	Rick and the Socks
	Time, Talent, Treasure
Strength (for living)	*The Outboard Motor*
Success	*A Ball Game*
Superficial Faith	*Christianity Lite*
Support	*The Choir Member*
Ten Commandments	*The Ten Guidelines*
Third World	*$325.00*
Tithing	*Let's Make a Tithe Deal*
	Rick and the Socks
Transformation	*Raising a Dad*
	Some Paint and Wallpaper
Walk (Christian walk)	*The Shoe Store*
Word of God	*The Road Trip*
	The Christian Plant
World Relief	*$325.00*
Special Days	
Christmas	*All I Want for Christmas*
	Mary's Story
	Whose Party?
Palm Sunday	*On Location! With Brock Tully*
Pentecost	*The Guide*
	The Outboard Motor
Stewardship Sunday	*Let's Make a Tithe Deal*
	Rick and the Socks
	Time, Talent, Treasure
Super Bowl Sunday	*The Greatest Bowl Game of All — Life*

ABOUT THE AUTHOR

Paul Lessard is a writer, dramatist and musician. He has been involved in the creative communication of faith through worship, pulpit dramas, puppetry, and music for over 15 years. He has served two churches as Pastor of Worship and Drama and has led workshops on worship, drama and puppetry across the U.S. and Canada. Paul is one of the writers and puppeteers for the award-winning children's broadcast and video series "Quigley's Village." Paul has also been published by Group Publishing, Plastow Productions, JED Share, and numerous denominational magazines.

Paul, his wife Becky and their two children make their home in Prince Albert, Saskatchewan, Canada, where Paul teaches Drama, Music and Worship at Covenant Bible College.

If SERMONS ALIVE! inspired you to start a drama ministry,
you'll find everything you need to know in this
Meriwether Publishing book:

GETTING STARTED IN DRAMA MINISTRY

by
Janet Litherland

SERMONS ALIVE! made you realize that drama may
be used to impart Christian truths in a fresh new way. You
want to incorporate more drama into your church's worship
services and programs, but you have some questions:

> **How may our plays be staged simply, yet effectively?**
>
> **Is there any way to get free advertising for our plays?**
>
> **How do we set up a church dinner theatre?**
>
> **Where are additional resources to help us in setting up
> a drama ministry?**

GETTING STARTED IN DRAMA MINISTRY answers
these questions and more. This guidebook is more than a
compilation of plays or a rehash of religious drama history.
It deals directly with drama in Christian education and
worship, for fun and for fellowship. It gives practical pointers
on raising funds, acting, directing, and all other aspects of
church drama. Also included are sample plays. This
paperback is available at your local Christian bookstore or
directly from the publisher: **Meriwether Publishing Ltd.,
P.O. Box 7710, Colorado Springs, CO 80933.**

You'll want to check out these additional sketches:

THE BEST OF THE JEREMIAH PEOPLE

by Jim Custer and Bob Hoose

SERMONS ALIVE! has brought out the actors in your congregation. Now they want to perform more sketches — on Sunday mornings, at retreats, camps, youth group meetings, Youth Sunday and other occasions. What better place to continue your drama ministry than with a book by America's leading Christian repertory group? **THE BEST OF THE JEREMIAH PEOPLE** is chock full of the group's trademark warm and forgiving satire with a "stinger" at the end. All sketches have been performance-tested through the Jeremiah People's twenty-plus successful years of touring nationwide. They also share their experience on rehearsing, theatre games, forms to help you set up a drama ministry, blocking, and managing lighting and sound on a budget.

Sample sketch titles include:

"A Typical Drive to Work?"

"Call Me Any Time"

"$685.00 Air Filter"

As with **SERMONS ALIVE!**, performance rights and permission to reproduce the sketches for your group are included with purchase of the book. This paperback is available at your local Christian bookstore or directly from the publisher: **Meriwether Publishing Ltd., P.O. Box 7710, Colorado Springs, CO 80933.**

ORDER FORM

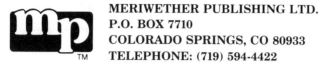 **MERIWETHER PUBLISHING LTD.**
P.O. BOX 7710
COLORADO SPRINGS, CO 80933
TELEPHONE: (719) 594-4422

Please send me the following books:

_____**Sermons Alive! #CC-B132**   **$14.95**
by Paul Neale Lessard
52 dramatic sketches for worship services

_____**Get a Grip! #CC-B128**   **$9.95**
by L. G. Enscoe and Annie Enscoe
Contemporary scenes and monologs for Christian teens

_____**The Best of the Jeremiah People #CC-B117**   **$14.95**
by Jim Custer and Bob Hoose
Humorous skits and sketches by leading Christian repertory group

_____**Christmas on Stage #CC-B153**   **$14.95**
by Theodore O. Zapel
An anthology of Christmas plays for performance

_____**Getting Started in Drama Ministry #CC-B154**   **$9.95**
by Janet Litherland
A complete guide to Christian drama

_____**Scripture Plays #CC-B150**   **$9.95**
by Dan Neidermyer
A book of plays dramatizing the Holy Bible

These and other fine Meriwether Publishing books are available at your local Christian bookstore or direct from the publisher. Use the handy order form on this page.

*I understand that I may return any book
for a full refund if not satisfied.*

NAME: _____

ORGANIZATION NAME: _____

ADDRESS: _____

CITY: _____ STATE: _____ ZIP: _____

PHONE: _____

☐ **Check Enclosed**
☐ **Visa or Mastercard #** _____

                                                        Expiration
Signature: _____ *Date:* _____
                    (required for Visa/Mastercard orders)

COLORADO RESIDENTS: Please add 3% sales tax.
SHIPPING: Include $1.50 for the first book and 50¢ for each additional book ordered.

☐ *Please send me a copy of your complete catalog of books and plays.*

ORDER FORM

MERIWETHER PUBLISHING LTD.
P.O. BOX 7710
COLORADO SPRINGS, CO 80933
TELEPHONE: (719) 594-4422

Please send me the following books:

_____**Sermons Alive! #CC-B132**   **$14.95**
by Paul Neale Lessard
52 dramatic sketches for worship services

_____**Get a Grip! #CC-B128**   **$9.95**
by L. G. Enscoe and Annie Enscoe
Contemporary scenes and monologs for Christian teens

_____**The Best of the Jeremiah People #CC-B117**   **$14.95**
by Jim Custer and Bob Hoose
Humorous skits and sketches by leading Christian repertory group

_____**Christmas on Stage #CC-B153**   **$14.95**
by Theodore O. Zapel
An anthology of Christmas plays for performance

_____**Getting Started in Drama Ministry #CC-B154**   **$9.95**
by Janet Litherland
A complete guide to Christian drama

_____**Scripture Plays #CC-B150**   **$9.95**
by Dan Neidermyer
A book of plays dramatizing the Holy Bible

These and other fine Meriwether Publishing books are available at your local Christian bookstore or direct from the publisher. Use the handy order form on this page.

I understand that I may return any book
for a full refund if not satisfied.

NAME: _____

ORGANIZATION NAME: _____

ADDRESS: _____

CITY: _____ STATE: _____ ZIP: _____

PHONE: _____

☐ **Check Enclosed**
☐ **Visa or Mastercard #** _____

*Signature:*_____   *Expiration*
                                                                    *Date:*_____

(required for Visa/Mastercard orders)

COLORADO RESIDENTS: Please add 3% sales tax.
SHIPPING: Include $1.50 for the first book and 50¢ for each additional book ordered.

☐ *Please send me a copy of your complete catalog of books and plays.*